E. Barnett

Archaeology
and
The Bible

Lieutenant Claude Regnier Conder, R. E., at Elisha's Spring (Jericho). (photo: PEF)

Archaeology
and
The Bible

Jonathan N. Tubb and Rupert L. Chapman

With a contribution by
Peter G. Dorrell

Published for the Trustees of the
British Museum
by British Museum Publications

© 1990 The Trustees of the British Museum

Published by British Museum Publications Ltd
46 Bloomsbury Street, London WC1B 3QQ

British Library Cataloguing in Publication Data
Tubb, Jonathan N.
    Archaeology and the Bible.
    1. Bible. Historicity. Archaeological sources
    I. Title   II. Chapman, Rupert L.
    III. British Museum *Trustees*
    220.93

ISBN 0–7141–1719–6

Designed by James Shurmer

Set in Bembo and printed in Great Britain
by The Bath Press, Avon

Photographs are reproduced by courtesy of the
following (sources are acknowledged by abbreviations
in the captions): Palestine Exploration Fund (PEF),
University College, London (UCL), Peter Dorrell/
Institute of Archaeology (PGD), Kathryn Walker
Tubb/Institute of Archaeology (KWT), Jonathan N.
Tubb (JNT), the Welcome Trust (WT) and the
Trustees of the British Museum (BM). Thanks are also
due to Ann Searight for drawing the maps and to
Molly Hunter for preparing the manuscript.

Front cover illustrations:
View from the west of Tell es-Sa'idiyeh in the Jordan
Valley and (*inset right*) excavating a grave at the site
(photos: JNT); engraving (*inset left*) showing members
of the Survey of Western Palestine, 1872–8 (PEF)

Contents

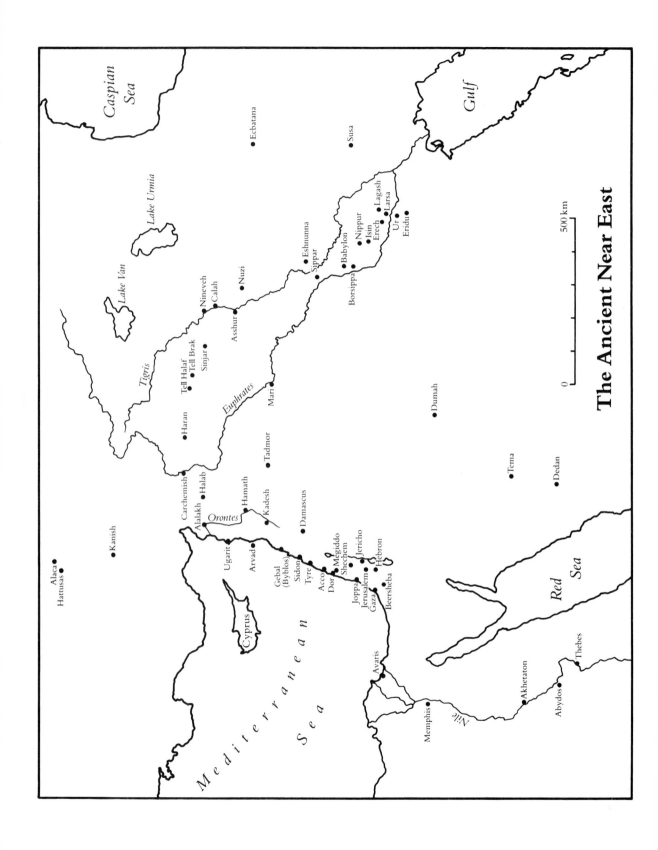

The Ancient Near East

Caspian Sea

Gulf

Lake Urmia

Lake Van

Ecbatana

Susa

Lagash
Erech Larsa
Nippur Ur
Isin Eridu
Eshnunna
Sippar
Babylon
Borsippa

Tigris

Nineveh
Calah
Asshur
Nuzi

Tell Halaf
Tell Brak
Sinjar

Euphrates

Mari

Haran

Dumah

Tadmor

Carchemish
Alalakh Halab
Hamath
Orontes Kadesh
Damascus

Kanish

Ugarit
Arvad
Gebal (Byblos)
Sidon
Tyre
Acco
Dor Megiddo
Shechem
Joppa Jericho
Jerusalem Hebron
Gaza Beersheba

Tema

Dedan

Alaca
Hattusas

Cyprus

Mediterranean Sea

Red Sea

Avaris

Memphis

Nile

Akhetaton

Abydos

Thebes

500 km

0

Preface

For more than 150 years biblical archaeology, that is, the branch of the archaeology of the Levant which focuses on the periods relating to the biblical narratives, has excited and inspired scholars and the general public alike with the possibility it offers of enhancing our understanding and enjoyment of the Bible through scientific research. Over the years since the early work of the Palestine Exploration Fund in the nineteenth century, ever increasingly refined techniques of excavation and recording, combined with subsidiary disciplines drawn from the natural and pure sciences, have led to a new and vital viewpoint from which it is possible to examine the events and characters of the biblical texts in an astonishingly detailed light.

Modern scholarship has fortunately rejected the tendency, prevalent during the early years of this century, to use archaeology as a tool for proving or disproving the validity of the Bible as an historical document. The Bible stands, as it always has done, not only as a wonderfully rich source of religious, historical and socio-philosophical material, the contents of which will allow any degree of analysis, but, first and foremost, as a magnificent work of literature. In these terms the question of proof or disproof can surely be seen as irrelevant.

Biblical archaeology today addresses itself to more appropriate issues, seeking to piece together the cultural and political history of the lands of the Bible, including the environmental, economic and demographic background. Through objective research its practitioners continue to make a real and invaluable contribution to our appreciation of the Bible.

Jonathan N. Tubb
Deir 'Alla, Jordan, March 1990

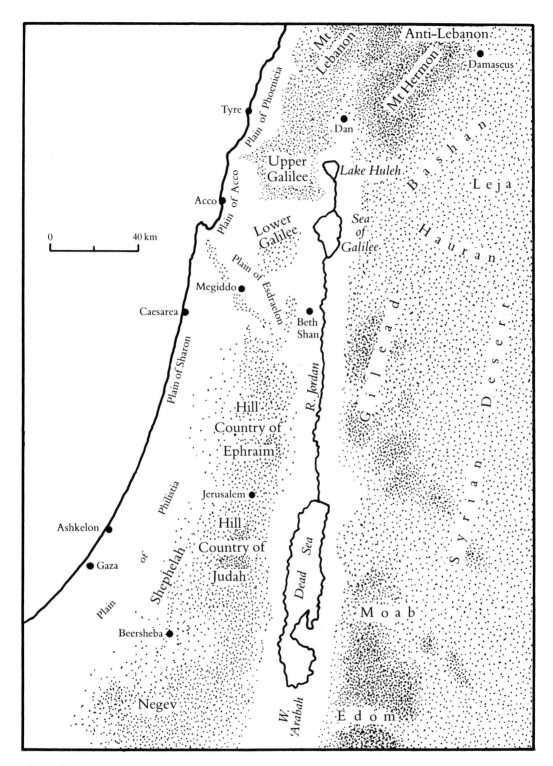

Map of the Levant showing geographical features.

Chapter 1
Pioneers of Biblical Archaeology
Rupert L. Chapman

'Go and explore the country and Jericho.' (Joshua 2:1)

From the time of William Tyndale, who produced the first English translation of the New Testament in 1526, and especially after the break with Rome, when in 1539 Henry VIII commissioned Bishop Miles Coverdale's translation for use in all English churches, there has been an important tradition of Bible reading in England. This tradition became steadily stronger through the sixteenth and seventeenth centuries, and the end of the eighteenth century saw a religious revival which strengthened it still further. This development was, however, matched by the revival of secular philosophy in the hands of Hobbes, Locke, Hume, and Berkeley in seventeenth- and eighteenth-century Britain. In the eighteenth century also began the challenge of 'secular humanism', which became a radical anti-religious movement in the French Revolution.

In science, the same century saw the work of Priestly and Boyle in chemistry, and Malthus' *Essay on the Principle of Population*, followed in 1859 by Darwin's *Origin of Species*, further advances in chemistry and physics, and the birth of modern geology, with its challenge to the traditional calculation of the age of the universe. Geography was greatly advanced by the search for new trade routes, markets, and sources of raw materials. In scholarship the nineteenth century saw the rise of the Tübigen school of biblical criticism, which broke with the tradition of religious exegetical scholarship. In Britain there were considerable social upheavals associated with the Industrial Revolution. This last development, however, produced the wealth which was quickly channelled into the many fields of enquiry opened by the new explorations of the world.

In this period archaeology developed, initially in Denmark, out of antiquarianism. There was a general rise of interest in the past, expressed in researches into the ancient history of many lands unconnected with the Bible or imperialism. The development of archaeology in the Holy Land sprang from this context. It is, however, interesting to note that few, if any, of the pioneers of British archaeology in the Holy Land had any background in the archaeology of Britain. The general teaching of Latin and Greek and the interest in Classical archaeology meant that most had a background in this area. Many also came from classical philology and from theology or biblical studies. Hence British archaeology in the Holy Land, like its American counterpart, must be seen as having developed largely independent of other regional archaeologies.

The first attempt at an accurate survey of the Holy Land was made during Napoleon's invasion in 1801, published as Jacotin's Map. Unfortunately, while this map depicts the whole of the country, it is only accurate for the territory actually held by Napoleon's army, which was the only area the surveyors could safely visit. The second attempt at an accurate survey of the entire Holy Land was made by a Dutch soldier, Lieutenant Van de Velde, and published in 1856, but although this survey did cover the entire country, Van de Velde worked alone and with limited funds so that his work was not completely accurate. Nevertheless it became the standard map until the publication of the Palestine Exploration Fund's *Survey of Western Palestine* in 1880.

In 1838 Edward Robinson, who had been appointed Professor of Biblical Literature at Union Theological Seminary, made a journey through the Holy Land to prepare himself to take up his post. His aim was to carry out a critical study of the historical geography of the country, and, in particular, to identify the sites mentioned in the Old Testament. In this he was outstandingly successful, and, in the two volumes of his *Biblical Researches in Palestine*, he laid the foundations of both the methodology and the conclusions of the modern studies of toponymy and historical geography in the Holy Land. In 1852 he made a second journey to complete his previous work, adding a third volume to his book.

In 1852 the Revd Arthur Stanley, later to become Dean of Westminster, travelled from Egypt through Sinai and toured Palestine. He published a book of his travels which became a Victorian bestseller. It was considerably more than a mere travelogue. Stanley was a careful observer, well acquainted with the Bible and Classical antiquity, and his book was a careful study of the relationship between biblical history and the geography of the lands in which that history took place. In order to make his study complete, he commissioned as an appendix a 'Vocabulary of Hebrew Topographical Words' by Mr George Grove, a civil engineer who was then the manager of the Crystal Palace and later became the founding Director of the Royal Academy of Music and author of the celebrated *Dictionary of Music*. While working on the Vocabulary, Grove recognised that, even after the work of Robinson, very little accurate and detailed information was known about the physical and historical geography of the Holy Land. As a result of the Vocabulary, Grove was asked in 1856 to write the articles dealing with Palestine for Dr William Smith's *Dictionary of the Bible*, which was intended to comprise all the information then known.

The Ordnance Survey of Jerusalem

From the time of his work on the *Vocabulary*, Grove appears to have been increasingly concerned with the problems of the historical geography of the Holy Land, and to have been biding his time and looking for an opportunity to organise some sort of expedition to study the subject on the ground. Through his many influential contacts he was able to seek political support and financial backing. Only a few years later an opportunity presented itself, and the first major scientific expedition, the Ordnance Survey of Jerusalem, was set in train. The following words by Colonel Sir Charles Watson from his *Fifty Years' Work in the Holy Land* tell us how the survey came to be organised:

One of Mr. Grove's coadjutors at the Crystal Palace was a well-known architect, the late Mr. James Fergusson, who was much interested in the topography of Jerusalem, especially as regards the Church of the Holy Sepulchre, and the site of the Temple of the Jews. Grove discussed with him the possibility of carrying out scientific research in Palestine, and frequently considered how researches of this nature could be set on foot, but nothing came of the idea for some years.

In 1864, the year after the publication of Smith's *Dictionary of the Bible*, an opportunity offered for the preparation of a survey of the city of Jerusalem. This was owing to the liberality of Miss Burdett-Coutts (the late Baroness Burdett-Coutts), who had her attention directed to the great want of a proper water supply for Jerusalem, and was anxious to assist in providing it. After enquiring as to the best way to begin, she learned that the first step was to have a good plan of Jerusalem and the surrounding country prepared, and decided to give £500 for the purpose, which was placed in the hands of Sir Henry James, then Director General of the Ordnance

1. General Sir Charles Wilson, K.C.M.B., R.E.
(photo: PEF)

Survey. Captain Wilson, R.E. (the late Major-General Sir C.W.Wilson, K.C.B.), offered his services, and, accompanied by a party of the Royal Engineers, proceeded to Palestine in June, 1864, to carry out the survey, which was satisfactorily completed in May, 1865.

Wilson describes the way in which he became involved in the Ordnance Survey of Jerusalem as follows:

The conditions were that £500 was to cover all expenses, including the passage out and home of the surveyors, and the preparation of the plans. An officer was to go, but he was to pay all his own expenses, and receive no extra pay whilst employed. The appointment was offered to several Royal Engineer officers, but the conditions were so hard, and the possibility of doing the work within the estimate considered to be so remote, that they all refused.

I happened to be in the room of one of the officers when he received the letter offering him the appointment; he said he would not go, and I then asked him, in writing his report, to say that I would go. I had only once seen Sir H.James before, and was therefore a little surprised when he accepted my offer. I was generally considered to be going on a fool's errand; many believed I would come to grief in money matters; and men who had previous experience in Palestine and Jerusalem told me they did not believe the Turkish officials would allow me to survey the city. The only man who gave me any encouragement and said he thought I had done right, was the late General H.D.Scott, R.E. I went out and surveyed not only the city, but the mosques and sacred area, and only exceeded the estimate by a few pounds, the excess being due to our being jammed in Egypt during the cholera epidemic of 1865.

The surveying team, consisting of Captain Wilson, Sergeant McDonald, and Corporals Ferris, McKeith, Davidson, and Wishart, all of the Royal Engineers, left Southampton on 12 September 1864, and arrived at Jaffa on 30 September:

where preparations had to be made for the journey to Jerusalem — a more troublesome matter than at the present time, when a train takes the traveller up to the capital in a few hours.

After spending a night in the Latin convent at Ramleh they started for Jerusalem, and Wilson described his first experience of Eastern travel in a letter home:—

'As we had a long journey before us, I determined to do it by night instead of travelling in the hot sun, so we started at half-past eleven p.m., taking under our protection six monks from the convent. After we had been out some time we got accustomed to the light, and found the air very cool and pleasant, the wind having changed round and bringing in a refreshing sea-breeze. After three and a half hours' riding we came to Latrun, and, immediately on leaving it, commenced ascending the mountains by a road which runs up a rocky gorge, and is, in fact, nothing but the dry bed of a mountain torrent, a rough sort of track being worn by a constant succession of horses. We were hardly aware of the badness of the road until daylight broke, and were then rather horrified to find the kind of path we had been going over in the dark.

'Much as I had heard and read about the country, I was quite unprepared for the wild desolation of the scene around us. It is like nothing else on earth, and baffles all description; hills that were once covered with vineyards are now nothing but a mass of rack and rubbish. We were passing close to the valley of Ajalon, where Joshua commanded the sun to stand still, and soon came to Kirjayth Jearim, where the road became even more wildly desolate, until we reached the summit of the last hill, and Jerusalem lay before us. I must say my first feeling was one of disgust, for, right in front, and hiding a great part of the city from this point of view, the

Russians have constructed an immense pile of ugly buildings, almost a town in itself, outside the walls.

'But other feelings came over me on looking down on a spot where such momentous events have taken place, and I do not believe that even an infidel or an atheist could view without emotion those few acres of ground where events happened which have had an ever-increasing influence over the actions of the whole human race.'

Captain Wilson and his party made their headquarters in the Prussian hospice, and Wilson made an immediate reconnaissance of the city and the surrounding territory. The following day, Wilson says:

The Consul and I went to pay the Governor [Izzet Pasha] an official visit, each preceded by a cavass in all the glory of beadledom. In the court we found the Turkish police drawn up to receive and salute us, and we were then ushered upstairs, His Excellency coming to the door to receive us, and giving us a European shake of the hand. Mr. Moore, the British Consul, is a perfect Turkish scholar, and was good enough to interpret for me. I found the Pasha very civil and liberal-minded, much more so than I had expected. He is well educated, seemed to take a great interest in what I was going to do, and promised to give me all the help he could.

Watson, who was Captain Wilson's friend as well as his biographer, describes the course of the work as follows:

Izzet Pasha was as good as his word, and issued strict orders to the inhabitants of Jerusalem that every facility was to be given to the survey party in the execution of the work. A suitable position for the base line was found on the plain of Raphaim, south-west of the city, and this was measured carefully three times with a standard chain, and the mean of these measurements, which were almost identical, was taken as the basis of calculation. A network of triangles, covering an area of 4½ miles in length, and 3 miles in breadth, was then extended from the base, the angles being observed with a seven-inch theodolite. The detail was afterwards filled in with a chain survey of the ground on the outskirts of the city, and a traverse survey of the streets made with a five-inch theodolite.

Wilson also obtained permission to make an accurate survey of the sacred Haram area, the Dome of the Rock, and the Mosque of Aksa, sites from which, a few years previously, Christians had been rigorously excluded. He was rather anxious about this portion of the work, as it was the first time that surveying instruments had been allowed to be used by Christians in the Haram; but with his usual tact, he soon set up a strong friendship with the Sheikh of the Holy Place, whose family are said to have held the right of guardianship since the time that Saladin recaptured Jerusalem from the Crusaders in the twelfth century, and was allowed to work, without let or hindrance, wherever he wished.

On 30 November Wilson wrote home concerning his mission:

The work goes on slowly, as the country is rough and difficult, and will keep us out here much longer than we expected. I have been doing a great deal of underground work lately, and have been rewarded by several discoveries, the most important being an entire arch of one of the approaches to the Temple in a beautiful state of preservation, and a fine portion of the old wall. It is rather dirty work, crawling about in the middle of the earth, but very interesting.

Last week I made an expedition with Dr. Chaplin through a passage cut in the solid rock to conduct the water from the Kedron Valley into the Pool of Siloam. At first we were able to stand up, but were soon brought down to our hands and knees, and for some distance had to lie down on our sides and wriggle along like eels: not a comfortable sort of locomotion at any time, but when it has to be done in six inches of water and mud, dreadfully unpleasant. There was just room between the water and the top of the passage to carry our heads along and breathe. I was leading, and managed to carry my candle through in safety, but Dr. Chaplin lost his, and got several mouthfuls of dirty water in forcing his way through.

I find much less difficulty than I expected in getting about to different places, and, from working quietly at first, have established a sort of right to go wherever I like, and the inhabitants are now quite accustomed to see my head suddenly appearing out of wells and cisterns. The greatest difficulty I have is in getting into the interior of private houses, especially amongst the Jews, and they live just in the place where I want to work, in what is called by Josephus the Lower City.

Wilson and his team made what is still the most accurate plan of the Church of the Holy Sepulchre. They also ran a line of levels from the Mediterranean to the Dead Sea, in order to determine the difference of level between the two for the first time with scientific accuracy. Although there had been many individual explorers and travellers, the Ordnance Survey of Jerusalem was the first major, purely scientific expedition to attempt the survey of a portion of the Holy Land.

Foundation of the Fund

The success of the Ordnance Survey of Jerusalem, and the public attention which it attracted, convinced George Grove that the time was ripe to establish a society for the scientific exploration of Palestine. The Very Revd A.P. Stanley, Dean of Westminster, provided the Jerusalem Chamber, Westminster, for a meeting on 12 May 1865. It was presided over by the Archbishop of York and attended by a number of people interested in the proposed society. The meeting passed the following resolution:

That an Association be formed, under the title of the Palestine Exploration Fund, for the purpose of investigating the Archæology, Geography, Geology, and Natural History of Palestine.

Mr. G. Grove was appointed Honorary Secretary, while Mr. J. A. Smith, M.P., and Mr. R.C. Hanbury, M.P., were appointed Treasurers. A Sub-Committee, consisting of the Archbishop of York, the Dean of Westminster, and Professor Owen, were entrusted with the task of drawing up a statement explaining the objects of the Society and appealing to the public for funds to carry out those objects.

The preliminaries having been thus arranged, a public meeting was held in Willis's Rooms on June 22nd, 1865, under the presidency of the Archbishop of York, when the Society was formally constituted.

In his opening address the Archbishop laid down certain principles on which, he said, the work of the Society would be based. These were:—

1. That whatever was undertaken should be carried out on scientific principles.
2. That the Society should, as a body, abstain from controversy.
3. That it should not be started, nor should it be conducted, as a religious society.

In 1915 Col. Sir Charles Watson, then Chairman of the Fund, wrote: 'The object of the first principle was to ensure that the results of inquiry and exploration should command from the world the same acceptance as a new fact reported from a physical laboratory, and that the work should be faced in the same spirit of fearless investigation into the truth as obtains in scientific research.'

While it is clear that many of the founders of the Fund hoped that archaeology and other scientific research would buttress the historicity of the biblical account of history, it is also equally clear that their interests were not limited by that biblical account. More important was the fact that *they were prepared to seek the truth concerning the past of the Holy Land, whether it supported their own interpretation of the biblical account or not.* Until the major field efforts of the American Schools of Oriental Research (founded in 1900), which did not begin until after the First World War, the Palestine Exploration Fund was the single most active learned society specialising in the study of the Holy Land. It was also a very popular organisation, with branches in various cities in Britain as well as a branch in the United States. Following the foundation of the Fund, a multitude of similar societies was set up in various countries, among which there has always been both friendly rivalry and close co-operation. Over the years these societies have established a distinguished record both in scholarly research and in making the results of this research available as quickly as possible to the general public.

Wilson's 'Reconnaisance of the Land' for the Fund

When Captain Wilson returned to London, the newly formed Committee immediately applied for his services to carry out, as Watson put it in 1915, 'such a preliminary survey as would enable the Committee to fix on suitable places for future exploration, and also to acquire such special information as would throw light upon the different points referred to in the original prospectus' of the Fund. Captain Wilson, Lieutenant Anderson, R.E., with Corporal Phillips and the rest of the enlisted men, landed at Beirut on 22 November 1865, and travelled eastward to Baalbek and Damascus, taking photographs and astronomic and trigonometric measurements as they went. At the village of Harran el Aramid, Corporal Phillips' photographic developing tent was stolen by the villagers, and he had to make a new one in order to continue his work. With the help of the Turkish authorities, Wilson was able to gain access to and plan the Ummayad Mosque at Damascus. From here they travelled to Banias, at the head of the Jordan, where they began their main work on 1 January 1866. They followed the Jordan down past Lake Huleh to the Sea of Galilee, where they investigated Tell Hum, the site of New Testament Capernaum, Khan Minyeh, Mejdel, New Testament Magdala, home of Mary of Magdala, and Tiberias. Because the governor of Tiberias was unwilling to give the survey party an escort to protect them from the bedu, who were in rebellion against the Turkish authorities at that time, they were unable to examine the eastern shore of the Sea of Galilee or the Jordan Valley. They set out westwards to Nazareth, surveying the hills of Galilee. From here they went south to the Plain of Jezreel, and east to Beisan, biblical

Beth Shan, and on to Nablus, ancient Neapolis, near the site of biblical Shechem and mounts Gerizim and Ebal, the mounts of 'Blessing' and 'Cursing', on the first of which Captain Wilson excavated a Byzantine church. Here a rumour that treasure had been found led to an attempt to loot the party's tents. The attack was repulsed, and the Turkish governor provided a military escort to prevent similar accidents. The party reached Jerusalem in April 1866, where it terminated its work and returned to England.

Warren's Expedition to Jerusalem

The results of Wilson's preliminary survey showed the magnitude of the task. The Fund was not financially prepared for an operation on this scale. It was decided that work in Jerusalem would be a preliminary option which would both show results and assist in raising public interest and money for the great project of mapping the land.

The difficulties of the work proved to be considerably greater than had been the case with previous expeditions. The expedition consisted of Lieutenant Charles Warren (later General Sir Charles Warren, G.C.M.G.), Corporal Phillips (who was again in charge of photography), Corporal Birtles (who was in charge of the excavations) and Corporal Hancock (who was to complete the Ordnance Survey). In the first instance the firman or letter of permission from the Turkish government did not arrive on time, and when it did, it had confused Hebron with Jerusalem, and expressly forbade Warren from doing any work within the Haram esh-Sheriff, or Noble Sanctuary. Warren was advised by Mr Moore, the British Consul, not to present it, so the letter was returned to Constantinople for revision and correction. In the meantime Izzet Pasha, the Turkish civil governor of Jerusalem, gave Warren permission to work anywhere except within the Noble Sanctuary itself. Warren and his team accordingly began work outside the southern wall of the Haram. Unfortunately the military governor, an elderly and devoutly religious man, opposed the work and ordered it stopped on the grounds that it would undermine the walls of the Haram. In fact, this was only a pretence, for his firm belief was that the folklore concerning the Haram itself and the city of Jerusalem contained all necessary truth, and therefore it was unnecessary for the Christians to come and dig there. Eventually, however, Warren was able to win him over, and the work went on.

In March 1867 Izzet Pasha was replaced as civil governor by Nazif Pasha, who took great offence at the work of the expedition and began to order them to stop work at each site as they began it. Eventually he forbade Warren to work closer than 40 ft to the walls. Warren evaded this restriction by sinking his shafts at the required distance from the walls, and then mining up to them, which the Pasha did not appear to realise was within the team's capacity. In June 1867 Warren carried out a reconnaissance of northern Transjordan, during which he took some of the earliest photographs of this area. The difficulties with Nazif Pasha culminated in an incident in which Sergeant Birtles was arrested. This gave Warren an opportunity to threaten to create a diplomatic incident, effectively neutralising the Pasha and enabling the expedition to proceed with its work. Later, junior officials attempted to extract bakhshish, effectively bribes, from

2. Lieutenant Charles Warren (later General Sir Charles Warren, G.C.M.G.) with Jakoob esh-Shellaby at Nablus. (photo: PEF)

Warren and the landowners on whose property he worked, to whom he paid compensation for disruption. Again Warren was able to overcome this opposition by simply refusing to comply with their demands.

In April 1868 Corporals Duncan and Hanson arrived to join the expedition, and Sergeant Birtles was sent home on medical leave. At this time Warren felt obliged to report personally to the Committee in London the real difficulties he was encountering in Jerusalem. He left Thomas Chaplin, a British Doctor, resident in Jerusalem, in charge of the work and returned to London. There he insisted that more funds were required, and that more overseers should come out with Sergeant Birtles. Warren then returned to Jerusalem with his family. On 10 August 1868 Corporal Duncan died of fever – possibly malaria, a constant affliction for the expedition – and was buried in the British Cemetery. On 10 September Sergeant Birtles, Corporal Turner, Corporal Cock, Corporal McKenzie and one other non-commissioned officer arrived. Corporal Turner was invalided home in November. Although relations with the Pasha had greatly improved and the work was able to continue, Warren was repeatedly forced to counter claims for damages against the Fund based on the ground that their work was undermining the foundations of various houses.

All of these difficulties were additional to the difficulties of the work itself, which was extremely dangerous. Warren's method of working was to sink deep shafts from which galleries would be run to follow walls, passages, etc., a method of working which today is considered to be both unproductive and destructive of evidence. Warren wrote of the work that:

... we were frequently subject to being blown up by the loose shingle which in an instant would destroy our galleries; to being smashed by the large pieces of masonry which lay huddled together above us, loosely lying one over the other, and ready to collapse at the slightest movement beneath them; or else to having our skulls stove in by the stones and iron bars which the fellahîn, in their anxiety to be smart, occasionally allowed to fall back on us from the mouth of the shafts.... Both within and without, but more particularly in the Tyropœon Valley within, the soil is impregnated with some poisonous matter, probably very ancient sewage; and whenever we scraped skin off our hands, instead of healing up at once the wound would sicken, and in a few days fester up; so that when we were first working at Robinson's Arch, above the pavement, our hands were continually sore; but below the pavement the earth appeared to be sound.

On one occasion, while clearing a passage beneath the single gate in the southern wall of the Haram, Sergeant Birtles was trapped for two hours by a fall of stone.

In spite of all of these difficulties, however, Warren and his men succeeded in discovering most of the information presently available to us concerning the details of the construction of the Haram esh-Sheriff, Herod's Temple Platform, and revealed a massive amount of information concerning the topography of Jerusalem prior to the build-up of debris which has produced the present surface. In addition, a substantial quantity of antiquities was recovered, although as yet no means of dating these was available for materials predating the Classical period.

Holland and Palmer's exploration of the Desert of the Exodus

In 1869, as the result of the successes of Wilson and Warren and a fund-raising drive by the Revd Pierce Butler, of Ulcombe, Kent, an expedition commanded by Captain Wilson was mounted under the auspices of the Ordnance Survey to survey the possible routes of the Exodus in the southern Sinai peninsula, with the remit to ascertain the answers to several specific questions. In particular, they were to attempt to decide whether Jebel Serbal, in the south of the peninsula, or Jebel Musa, the traditional site, better fitted the biblical account of Mt Sinai. Captain Wilson was assisted by Captain H.S.Palmer, R.E.; the Revd F.W.Holland, Hon. Secretary of the Palestine Exploration Fund; Professor E.H.Palmer, of St John's College, Cambridge; and Mr Wyatt, a naturalist; and four non-commissioned officers of the Royal Engineers, of whom Sergeant-Major MacDonald was expedition photographer.

The expedition left Suez on 11 November 1868, and completed the survey of the south-western portion of the peninsula, between the central plateau and the sea, by April 1869. In the conditions of that time – no roads of any kind, only desert trails

3. Members of the Sinai Survey team (*left to right*): guides Hassan and Salem, Professor E. H. Palmer, Captain H. S. Palmer, Captain C. W. Wilson, the Revd F. W. Holland and Mr C. Wyatt. (photo: PEF)

– and travelling entirely by camel, this was a very considerable achievement. Their conclusion was that Jebel Serbal could not have been the mountain described in the Bible, but that Jebel Musa could. They believed that this settled the argument once and for all, and that the traditional site was the true site. The argument has, however, continued, not only as to which mountain is the one described, but as to whether the events took place at all. While the latter argument is as far from an agreed conclusion as ever, it does seem increasingly likely that Captain Wilson and his team were correct in identifying Jebel Musa as the mountain described in the biblical account. A number of their other site identifications have stood the test of critical examination for over 120 years, a considerable tribute to these early explorers.

Following the success of the Ordnance Survey of Sinai, the need was felt for a survey of the Desert of the Wanderings in northern Sinai. For this purpose the Palestine Exploration Fund engaged Professor Palmer, and Mr C. F. Tyrwhitt Drake (also of Cambridge), who was to report on the natural history of the region. These two travelled without servants and without guides or escort, other than the camel drivers, carrying their very limited baggage. They had to change these drivers as they passed from one tribal area to another. They left Suez on 16 December 1869 and reached Jebel Musa on 28 December, from whence they proceeded to 'Ain Hudeirat. In this region they found large numbers of round stone 'huts', called 'nawamis' by the bedu. These are now known to be tombs of the fourth millennium BC.

From here they proceeded north through eastern Sinai to Nakhl, a way-station on the pilgrim road between Egypt and the Hejaz. They then followed Wadi el-Arish north-wards to Wadi Kadeis, which they followed to 'Ain Qadeis, probably Kadesh Barnea, where the Israelites lived for a number of years during their wilderness wanderings. From 'Ain Qadeis they entered the Negev, visiting the ruins of a number of Byzantine cities including El Aujeh (ancient Nessana), Esbaita, and Khalasa (ancient Elusa). They then went to Beersheba, Hebron and Jerusalem.

On a second expedition, they went south from Hebron to Wadi Arabah and Mt Hor. Then Palmer turned east to Petra and north through Moab, visiting Dibon, Jericho, and the Dead Sea on the way back to Jerusalem, where he made a careful study of the Dome of the Rock.

Palmer and Tyrwhitt Drake's pioneering work showed the need for a more thorough survey of this area, but this was not to be carried out until 1914. In 1882, when travelling through Sinai as an agent of the British government, Professor Palmer and his party were attacked and murdered – a sad illustration of the risks taken by these pioneers for the sake of archaeology.

The Survey of Western Palestine

The aim of the Fund from its foundation had been to carry out an accurate and detailed survey of the whole of the Holy Land. In June 1871 an appeal for funds was made, and Captain R.W.Stewart, R.E., was appointed to command the expedition, with Sergeant Black and Corporal Armstrong as his assistants. The party landed at Jaffa in November 1871 and immediately laid out a base line, four miles in length, near Ramleh, and began setting up the trigonometric stations for the triangulation of the topographic survey. Within a few weeks, however, Captain Stewart was 'attacked by fever', probably malaria which was endemic at the time, and had to be sent back to England. Tyrwhitt Drake, along with Sergeant Black, took over the running of the survey and continued the work pending the arrival of a replacement for Captain Stewart. In July 1872 Lieutenant Claude Regnier Conder joined the survey party at Nablus. As Watson wrote in 1915, 'Up to that time 560 square miles of country had been surveyed, and Conder found that the work, both as regards triangulation and plans, had been most satisfactorily carried out by the non-commissioned officers under the superintendence of Mr. Drake.' The surveyors took careful notes of the place-names, all geographical features, the archaeology, and the demography of the country. Perhaps the most succinct account of the progress of the work is that given by Watson in 1915:

The work of the survey was conducted on a regular system which improved as time went on. The party consisted of five Europeans and six native servants and assistants, together with a soldier supplied as escort by the local government. For transport there were eight horses and seven mules with half a dozen camels for carrying the tents and camp equipage. On arriving at a place judged to be suitable for the survey of a certain district, the first duty was to select a good camping ground, sheltered from the wind and provided with water. Then negotiations had to be made with the sheikh of the nearest village for the supply of provisions, and prices had to be fixed, often a matter entailing considerable bargaining. The first day after arrival at a new camp was usually devoted to the selection of trigonometrical stations, and to the observation from these of the points previously fixed, after which the new points had to be picked up and fixed with the theodolite. As soon as the triangulation was satisfactorily completed, the filling in of the topographical details was taken in hand, and the time taken for this varied with the nature of the country, as, in some parts, the difficulties were considerable, expecially in the mountainous districts, where there were valleys and rugged ravines of a thousand feet or more in depth.

Ruins were often hidden in corners, and half-way down precipitous descents, when it took hours to reach and examine them. Then the exact modern name of every village, hill, watercourse, ruin, etc., had to be ascertained and written in Arabic, no easy matter in a country where the same feature has sometimes several local names. It was hard work, necessitating constant attention on the part of Lieutenant Conder and his assistants.

By the end of 1872 an area of 1,250 square miles had been completed, and, as the work advanced, the monthly rate of progress increased, for experience showed improved methods of carrying out the survey. So far as the field operations were concerned, all went on satisfactorily, but the Committee found it by no means easy to keep up the supply of money in order to meet the many expenses, and this caused the work to take longer than would have been necessary had it been possible to increase the strength of the survey party.

The country mapped during the first two years of the survey included the area embraced between the sea coast, and a line drawn north and south from Nazareth to Jerusalem. In the autumn of 1873 Lieutenant Conder began work on the southern part of Palestine, the scene of the battles between the Israelites and Philistines, and the territory governed by the kings of Judah. Then, in November, the surveyors moved down into the valley of the Jordan, where they met with a serious check, as Conder and Drake, together with others of the party, were attacked by the fever, which makes the vicinity of Jericho so unhealthy, and it was not until February, 1874, that the work could be resumed and pushed up the Jordan valley towards the Sea of Galilee.

In May, 1874, Conder came to England on leave and gave a full account of the progress of the survey at the Annual Meeting of the Society. During his absence from Palestine, Mr. Drake was again taken ill, and died at Jerusalem, to the great regret of the Committee, as the services which he had rendered had been most valuable, and his knowledge of Arabic had caused him to be greatly respected by the Arabs and native authorities. His place on the survey was taken by Lieutenant H. H. Kitchener, R.E. (now Earl Kitchener of Khartoum), who joined the party in November, and the work was carried on steadily until June, 1875, by which time an area of more than 4,400 square miles had been completed.

In the following month, when the survey was making excellent progress in Northern Palestine, a serious attack was made on the party by the inhabitants of Safed, a large town in the hills above the Sea of Galilee, and the two officers, together with a number of the staff and servants, were seriously injured with sticks and stones. A report was made to the Foreign Office through the Consul-General at Beirut, and it was decided to stop the work until the culprits had been tried and punished. The trial was held at Acre, and the ringleaders were imprisoned, while a sum of £150 was levied on the town of Safed.

The proceedings in connexion with this attack occupied a considerable time, and while these were in progress, the survey party remained in London, and worked diligently at drawing the map and preparing the reports for publication. The amount of valuable material which had been brought home by Lieutenant Conder far surpassed the expectations of the Committee and gave evidence of the labour, zeal, and intelligence which he had devoted to the work. A Special Survey Publication Committee was appointed to examine and collect the whole of these materials, and Captain Wilson and Mr. Grove were nominated as general editors of the Memoirs, with Captain Anderson as sub-editor of the map, which it was decided to publish in twenty-six sheets,

4. Lieutenant
H. H. Kitchener, R. E. (later
Lord Kitchener). (photo:
PEF)

on the scale of one inch to the mile, together with a second edition of the map on a smaller scale for the use of travellers and Bible students.

Early in 1877, after the trial of the Safed people had terminated satisfactorily, it was arranged that Conder should remain in London and complete the preparations for publication, while Kitchener and the field party returned to Palestine to finish what remained of the survey of Galilee. Starting at Haifa, early in March, the party reached Safed in April, and were welcomed by the inhabitants, who expressed their sorrow for what had taken place on the previous occasion. The survey was then pushed on rapidly and was finally completed in September, 1877, having taken a little less than six years to carry out, including the delay caused by the unfortunate affair at Safed. The map, when completed, was photo-lithographed by the Ordnance Survey at Southampton and published in 1880, while, in the years 1881–84, the Committee published the great work entitled the *Survey of Western Palestine*, edited by the Secretary, Mr. Walter Besant. This was the most important work on the Holy Land ever given to the world, and the most valuable contribution to the illustration of the Bible since its translation into the vulgar tongue. The work was comprised in seven volumes, containing:—

1. The Memoirs, in three volumes, containing the drawings, plans, sketches, and notes made by the survey officers, supplemented by such other information as could be obtained from authentic sources.

2. The Name Lists, containing more than 10,000 names collected during the survey, transliterated and translated by Lieutenant Conder and edited by Professor Palmer.

3. The Special Papers, being a reproduction of papers which had already appeared in the *Quarterly Statements*.

4. The Jerusalem volume, giving a complete account of the excavations by Captain Warren, together with a description of other researches in the Holy City by Captain Wilson, Lieutenant Conder, Monsieur Gannaeu, Dr. Chaplin, Dr. Schick, etc.

5. The Flora and Fauna of Palestine, by the Rev. Canon Tristram, F.R.S.

This is undoubtedly the largest project ever carried out by the Palestine Exploration Fund, and possibly its greatest contribution. The true value of the mass of information collected in those six years is only now being fully recognised, as awareness grows of the extent of the changes which have taken place since 1880, and of the importance of such changes to our understanding of the events of the more distant past.

The Survey of Eastern Palestine

In 1870 the American Palestine Exploration Society was formed in emulation of the Palestine Exploration Fund. It was a more openly religious organisation, and lacked the express commitment to scientific objectivity of the British organisation. Friendly communications were immediately established between the two groups, and it was agreed that the Americans would be responsible for the survey of Eastern Palestine. Owing to the prevailing political conditions, this was a more difficult area to deal with, and the American organisation lacked the pool of experience represented by the Ordnance Survey of the Royal Engineers, on which the British organisation was able to draw. Their survey party, led by Lieutenant Edgar Z. Steever, arrived at Haifa in February 1873, from whence, after a short stay with Conder and the British survey party, they proceeded to Transjordan to begin work. The results of their work were very disappointing, owing to the differing natures of the British and American surveys, and to the many inaccuracies produced in the American map due to lack of experience and poor methods. Although results somewhat more comparable to those of Conder and the British party were later achieved for the description of the country by Revd Selah Merrill, his lack of academic background meant that even this relative success suffered by comparison.

In view of the failure of the American effort (the APES was disbanded in 1884), the Palestine Exploration Fund decided to carry out its own survey of Eastern Palestine. Lieutenant Conder was again to be in charge, assisted by Lieutenant A.M.Mantell, R.E., and sergeants Black and Armstrong, who had assisted in the Survey of Western Palestine. Landing at Beirut in March 1881, Conder began by visiting the valley of the Orontes, and identifying the site of the ancient city of Qadesh-on-Orontes, where a famous battle between Ramesses II of Egypt and the Hittites took place, with Tell en-Neby Mendoh.

Because of the political conditions in Transjordan, the party was not able to begin work until August. Work was begun in the area south of the ruins of Philadelphia, biblical Rabbath Ammon, later the site of modern Amman, with a base line laid out between Heshbon and Madaba. Conder devoted much attention to the dolmens, or megalithic tomb-chambers, and the menhirs, or single standing stones, found in large fields in this area of Transjordan as well as in the Golan to the north. All seemed set for the sort of successful results which had already been achieved west of the Jordan, but this was not to be. As Watson wrote in 1915:

All seemed to be going on well for a time until the Turkish Governor of Es Salt refused to allow the survey to proceed, and, as any attempt to act in opposition to his orders might have led to serious results, Conder and the party were obliged to return to Jerusalem, but, fortunately 500 square miles of country had been surveyed, and a large quantity of useful information had been collected before the work was stopped. Application was made to the Turkish Government at Constantinople for a new firman, but without success, although promises were given that it would be granted under certain conditions. The time of waiting was employed in working up the materials which had been collected and preparing them for publication.

The results were published in 1883 as the *Survey of Eastern Palestine*, Volume I. Sadly, this was the only volume of the series which was ever to appear. The work of the survey of Eastern Palestine was later continued for the Fund by Dr Gottlieb Schumacher, a German engineer employed on the survey of the line of the railway from Haifa to Damascus, and his work in the Hauran and the Jaulan was published in 1886, while a further survey carried out by Schumacher in the area of northern Ajlun was published in 1889.

Kitchener and Hull: The Wadi Arabah Survey

One of the special interests of the founders of the Palestine Exploration Fund was the geological exploration of the land. With this aim, and the aim of further adding to the Map of Western Palestine, an expedition was organised in 1883 comprised of Professor Edward Hull, F.R.S., the Director of the Geological Survey of Ireland, his son, Dr E. Gordon Hull, who was a skilled photographer, Mr H. C. Hart, a botanist and naturalist, and Mr R. Lawrence, Associate of the Royal College of Science, Dublin, who acted as meteorologist. As surveyor Captain H. H. Kitchener was assisted by Mr George Armstrong, who, as Corporal, and later Sergeant, Armstrong, had taken part in the Survey of Western Palestine. They left Suez in November 1883, travelling down the western side of the Sinai peninsula, via Serabit el-Jemel and Wadi Nasb, then up the eastern side of Sinai to 'Aqaba, which they reached late in November. They then surveyed the Wadi Arabah from 'Aqaba to the Dead Sea. The geological survey was then continued westwards to Beersheba, where Kitchener returned to duty in Egypt. After a long spell in quarantine in Gaza, the rest of the party continued the geological survey northwards to Jaffa and Jerusalem. From here they proceeded to the Jordan Valley and the Dead Sea. Much of great value about the geological history of the land was revealed by this expedition, including the history of the varying levels of the Dead Sea, and the fact that the Wadi Arabah was a major geological fault. It is now known to form a part of the crustal rift system, extending southwards down the Gulf of 'Aqaba, and into Africa,

5. Members of the Wadi Arabah Survey (*left to right*): George Armstrong, Professor Edward Hull, H. C. Hart, Dr E. Gordon Hull and Captain H. H. Kitchener. (photo: PEF)

where it becomes the Great Rift Valley, and northwards into Lebanon, where it becomes the Beqa. Much information was also gathered concerning the fossils from the various strata, and about the history of vulcanism in Sinai and in the Hauran and Jebel Druze. Professor Hull published two books as a result of this expedition, *Mount Seir, Sinai, and Western Palestine*, and, in the *Survey of Western Palestine* series, *The Geology of Palestine and Arabia Petræa*.

The Beginnings of Scientific Excavation: Petrie and Bliss at Tell el-Hesy

In 1894 the great historical geographer, the Revd George Adam Smith, wrote in the preface to the first edition of his monumental *Historical Geography of the Holy Land*, 'The exploration of Western Palestine at least, is almost exhausted on the surface, but there is a great future for it under-ground. We have run most of the questions to earth: it only remains to dig them up.' The first modern archaeological excavation in the Holy Land, on behalf of the Palestine Exploration Fund, began exactly 100 years ago this year, in 1890. The archaeologist chosen by the Fund to carry out this excavation was William Matthew Flinders Petrie, later Sir Flinders Petrie, who had already done a great deal of pioneering work in Egypt.

Throughout the Levant the modern traveller will find numerous curious small hills, which jut up abruptly from the general landscape. In the semitic-speaking countries these are referred to as 'tell', or 'khirbet', and the Turkic speaking countries 'tepe', or 'huyuk'. In the years of the early exploration of the Holy Land these were thought to be natural features of the landscape. Only with the work of Heinrich Schliemann at Hisarlik in 1871–1873 was it realised that these 'hills' were actually mounds of ruins. In the Holy Land, and throughout the rest of the Near East until the last few years, most buildings were constructed of unbaked mud-brick. When such a building eventually falls into decay the materials cannot be easily re-used, so it is simpler to level the remains and build again, using fresh mud-brick. Since the factors which make a site desirable tend to remain constant over long periods, occupation on a particular site tends to continue for a very long time, in some cases for as long as eight thousand years. As buildings fall into decay and new ones are constructed the level of the surface of the site rises, until an entirely man-made hill is created: a 'tell'. These tells were to be the new focus of attention for those carrying out research into the history and prehistory of the Holy Land.

When, in 1890, a permit to excavate was obtained by the Fund from the Turkish authorities, the area chosen contained two sites, Khirbet Ajlan and Umm Lakis, then thought to be biblical Eglon, one of the cities of the Philistine pentapolis, and Lachish, an important city of the kingdom of Judah. When Petrie was able to begin work in the area of the permit, he discovered that the earliest remains at Khirbet Ajlan and Umm Lakis were Roman. About two miles south of Khirbet Ajlan, however, he found another site, Tell el-Hesy, which he concluded was the likely site of ancient Lachish (it is now thought to have been the site of ancient Eglon). Petrie proceeded to hire about thirty workmen and spent a six-week season putting down soundings at a number of points on the site.

Tell el-Hesy is unusual in one respect: the western side of the tell has been eroded away by the floodwaters which fill the Wadi Hesy each rainy season, leaving a natural cut, or section, through the entire depth of the layers which have resulted from the occupation history of the site. This allowed Petrie to obtain a sample of the pottery and artefacts which came from each of the successive layers without having to excavate an enormously deep trench. Imbued as he was with the evolutionary, or 'typological',

6. Professor
W. M. F. Petrie (later
Sir Flinders Petrie).
(photo: UCL)

thinking of the nineteenth century, he quickly recognised that, since the ordinary, undecorated pottery from each layer was different, it could be used as a guide to the age of the material from any layer on any site. Petrie was not slow to recognise the importance of his discovery, which, though not the first use of evolutionary typology, was the first application of the method to undecorated pottery (it had previously been applied to decorated Greek pottery, stone tools, coins, and metalwork). In his report on his work he was to state:

The excavations at Tell el-Hesy proved to be an ideal place for determining the history of pottery in Palestine. And once settle the pottery of a country, and the key is in our hands for all future explorations. A single glance at a mound of ruins, even without dismounting, will show as much to anyone who knows the styles of the pottery, as weeks of work may reveal to a beginner. At Tell el-Hesy there was a deep and stratified town to work on, and therefore good scope

7. Professor Frederick
Jones Bliss. (photo: PEF)

for dating by levels. And a clear section of the town had been cut open by the scouring of the torrent, so that any level could be worked in at once. In these happy circumstances a few weeks sufficed to obtain pottery of each age, from the Amorite [e.g., Early Bronze Age – R.L.C.] to the Greek times.

Using the criteria of stratification and the ceramic seriation which it provided, Petrie identified eleven successive 'cities', which he proceeded to date on the basis of the Egyptian objects which he found in the strata at Tell el-Hesy, and on the basis of the Palestinian artefacts which he had found in his excavations in Egypt, thus making one of the earliest uses of the principle of cross-dating, which he had already invented. Although Conder and some others rejected the use of pottery for dating purposes, Petrie's typically telegraphic report ultimately became the paradigmatic work for Levantine archaeology. Indeed, the American archaeologist W. F. Albright was later to say of the chronological conclusions of Petrie and Bliss at Tell el-Hesy that, 'The Petrie–Bliss chronology of 1894 was correct almost to the century as far back as about 1500 BC; before that the dates were much too low.'

Petrie had long since decided to devote his life to the study of ancient Egypt, and Palestinian archaeology held no lasting attraction for him, so at the end of his season at Tell el-Hesy he informed the Committee of the Fund that he wished to return to Egypt. As his successor the Fund chose an American, Dr Frederick Jones Bliss, the son of the Revd Dr Daniel Bliss, founder of what is today the American University of Beirut. Bliss had a thorough knowledge of Arabic, and, at Petrie's suggestion, spent a few weeks on Petrie's excavations in Egypt where Petrie taught him his methods of excavation and analysis. Bliss was obviously a 'quick study', since, on the basis of what would today be a scandalously brief training, he proceeded to carry out a much larger programme of excavations over a much longer time (from March 1891 until December 1892) with outstanding success, as witness Albright's comment quoted above. Bliss even added at least one innovation of his own, recording his finds in a 'site grid' of 5-ft squares, a procedure not taken up by his colleagues in Levantine archaeology or elsewhere until many years later. Bliss' results confirmed and expanded those of Petrie. In 'City III', Bliss found a clay tablet which bore a letter written in Akkadian cuneiform from an Egyptian official named Pa'pu to one of his superiors, complaining about the scheming of Zimreda, prince of Lachish, and Shipti-ba'lu who was to succeed him, to attack the territory of Canaanite princes loyal to the king of Egypt, and their attempt to discredit Pa'pu himself. This was the first of the letters from the diplomatic correspondence in the reign of Akhenaton to be discovered outside of Egypt. Bliss' work clearly showed the richness of the information which could be obtained by excavations in the Holy Land, and, with Petrie's report, provided a solid model and basis for further work.

Bliss and Dickie in Jerusalem

Following the success at Tell el-Hesy, the Fund decided to return to the important work of the archaeological exploration of Jerusalem, which had had such an exciting beginning in the work of Charles Warren. In the years immediately following Warren's work, the Fund had obtained the services of M. Charles Clermont-Ganneau, a French diplomat and antiquarian scholar, who had made an archaeological exploration of Western Palestine and of Jerusalem in the years 1871–1872, until he was forced to leave the country due to a complex plot by a German settler (later himself murdered by one of his own accomplices in the plot) involving allegations of the theft of antiquities at Gezer. This appears to have been brought on by Clermont-Ganneau's abrasive, somewhat arrogant, manner, and his diligence in exposing forged antiquities, in which his accuser appears to have had a hand. Clermont-Ganneau published two large volumes of the results of his antiquarian researches, which contain many valuable observations.

A great deal of research into the antiquities of Jerusalem was carried out for the Fund by Dr Conrad Schick, a German architect who was sent to Jerusalem by a Swiss missionary society in 1846, and remained to practise architecture until his death in 1901. In 1865 Captain Wilson encouraged Schick to begin examining the rock levels at Jerusalem and any antiquities, especially architecture. Dr Schick continued to report his many valuable observations until his death in 1901. Many of the structures which he observed have long since been removed, so that his is the only record which exists. He produced so many contributions to the *Palestine Exploration Fund Quarterly Statement* that they could not all be included, and the archives of the Fund are now beginning to yield some interesting 'delayed' results.

The Fund now engaged Bliss to continue the exploration of Jerusalem, which he did from 1894 until 1897, with the assistance of Mr Archibald C. Dickie, later Professor Dickie. By means of an extensive series of shafts and tunnels Bliss and Dickie explored the walls of Jerusalem, the rock levels, and the structures within the walls. The shafts and tunnels of Bliss and Dickie were not so deep as those of Warren, but there was still considerable danger. For example, in tracing the ancient city walls along the Kedron Valley, between the Pool of Siloam and the south-east corner of the Haram esh-Sheriff, as Watson recounts:

The exploration of this part of the wall, where it crossed the valley, was one of the most difficult tasks of the explorers, as the debris was very deep, one of the shafts having to be sunk for no less than 42 feet before the foundation was reached, and the rubbish was impregnated with sewage which had filtered through from the Old Pool, while the bottom of the shaft was filled with water.

In May, 1896, when Bliss and Dickie were returning to camp one evening after the conclusion of work, they were attacked by some drunken natives, and in the mêlée Dickie's arm was broken by a blow, an accident which necessitated his going to hospital for some weeks.

In spite of the difficulties and dangers, and in spite of methods which would not be permitted on scientific grounds today, Bliss and Dickie managed in the space of three years to accumulate a vast quantity of valuable information. Even today the book in which they reported their finds, and the archives containing a wealth of as yet unpublished additional information, which they left with the Fund, are of major interest to scholars studying Jerusalem. As Watson put it in 1915:

The results that had been gained were most satisfactory, as the course of the ancient [Roman and Byzantine – R.L.C.] south wall of Jerusalem and the position of its gates had been definitely settled, and the controversy regarding these points brought to a conclusion. The description of the historian Josephus had been proved to be correct, thus adding to the reliance that may be placed on his accounts of other matters connected with the topography of ancient Jerusalem.

Bliss and Macalister

The Committee of the Palestine Exploration Fund now decided to mount another tell excavation. F.J.Bliss was again appointed to excavate on behalf of the Fund, and Mr Dickie having returned to England, Mr R.A.Stewart Macalister, the son of Professor A.Macalister, professor of anatomy at Cambridge, was appointed as his assistant. A permit was obtained in 1898 for an area in the foothills of the central mountain range which contained four substantial sites which were excavated to varying extents.

The first of these sites was Tell Zakariyeh, which is, today, identified with biblical Azekah. It consisted of a lower tell and a higher citadel mound. The foundations of the citadel, which is now thought to date to the ninth or eighth century BC, were excavated and planned, and the line of the wall which had surrrounded the lower terrace, and is now dated to the tenth century BC, was also traced and planned. Shafts were sunk through the strata of the site to bedrock. The artefacts which they recovered are dated today to the Early Bronze Age (c.3500–c.1800 BC), the Middle and Late Bronze Ages (c.1800–1150 BC), and Iron Age I (c.1250–1000 BC), now generally recognised to be the period of the Exodus and the Judges, Iron Age II (c.1000–587 BC), the period of the Hebrew kings, and the Seleucid empire (fourth to first centuries BC).

From here Bliss and Macalister proceeded to Tell es-Safi, then and now identified as the site of the Philistine city of Gath. It consisted of a lower tell and a higher citadel mound, on which the Crusader king of Jerusalem, Fulke of Anjou, had constructed the castle of Blanche Garde. Most of the site was covered by the modern village, and much of the rest by two modern cemeteries, so that the area available for excavation was very limited. A series of shafts was sunk, to explore the stratigraphic history of the site, and the line of the fortifications was traced around the perimeter of the site. Here also the site appears to have been occupied throughout the Bronze and Iron Ages down to the Babylonian destruction of 587 BC, and was re-occupied from c.400–100 BC.

The third site to be tackled was Tell el-Judeideh, now identified as the biblical town of Moresheth-Gath, near the modern town of Beit Jibrin (now known as Bet Guvrin). Here Bliss and Macalister found Bronze Age remains, then a gap in occupation, followed by remains of the Iron II culture, and finally a massive system of fortifications, dated to the time of Herod the Great, with, in its centre, a *principia*, or headquarters building.

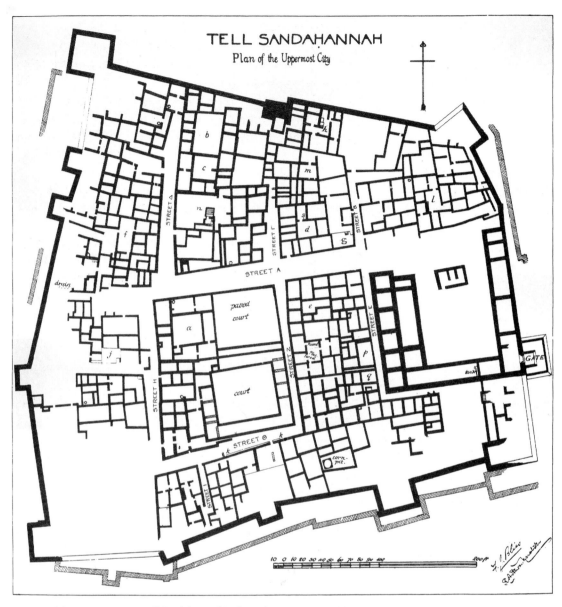

TELL SANDAHANNAH

Plan of the Uppermost City

8. Plan of the excavations at Tell Sandahanna(h), classical Marissa, one of four sites excavated by Bliss and Macalister between 1898 and 1900. (photo: PEF)

The final site tackled by Bliss and Macalister was Tell Sandahannah, biblical Mareshah, Classical Marisa. Here Bliss and Macalister uncovered the entire plan of the two uppermost, Hellenistic-Roman, strata. Beneath these strata they identified a third stratum, probably Iron II in date, which they did not explore. The Hellenistic city was laid out on the Hippodamian system, based on a grid of streets with blocks, or *insulae* of houses in between them. This was surrounded by a massive system of fortifications comprising a main curtain wall and an advance 'covering wall', or *proteichisma*, a system common in Greek fortifications, and with a long tradition in the Bronze and Iron Age military architecture of Palestine.

These sites were published in a major report volume by the Palestine Exploration Fund, which was followed by a smaller volume reporting the discovery of a remarkable painted tomb near the site. The excavations at these sites provided the largest corpus of artefacts yet made available to scholars interested in the archaeology of the Holy Land, and the fullness of the reporting shows the rapidly developing skill of Bliss as archaeologist. This was, however, to be the last excavation which he was to carry out in Palestine. For reasons which are not entirely clear the Fund decided to dispense with his services, and for its next venture he was replaced by his former assistant, R.A.S. Macalister.

Macalister at Gezer

The site chosen for the Fund's next excavation was Tell el-Jezari, biblical Gezer. The identification had been confirmed by M. Clermont-Ganneau's discovery of a series of inscriptions cut in the rock marking the boundaries of the property of Gezer. Macalister excavated here from 1902–1905 and again from 1907–1909, and cleared some 60 per cent of the large mound to bedrock. He identified some nine strata, as compared with the twenty-six strata identified in renewed excavations of the Hebrew Union College in 1964–73. He recovered a vast corpus of artefacts, which he published more fully than any previous excavator. Unfortunately he did not record the find-spots of any of the artefacts other than those which came from tombs, holding that all it was necessary for anyone to know of the find-spot of an artefact was the stratum from which it came. His notion of stratification was primitive, even for his own time, so that the strata which he identified were not well-defined, unitary bodies, but a mixture of architectural units from different phases, and, hence, a mixture of artefacts from different periods. Additionally, he chose to report the material in terms of social activities, rather than by stratum. Because of his antipathy for Bliss, Macalister chose to reject the terminology which they had used in the excavation of the four tells discussed above, and with it the dating of the artefacts. As a result, the American archaeologist W.F.Albright was later to observe, 'In fact, the archaeological chronology of Palestine was in some respects more obscure in 1914 than it had been two decades earlier.'

In 1909 Macalister was appointed Professor of Celtic archaeology in Dublin, and left Levantine archaeology.

Mackenzie at Beth Shemesh

In 1911 the Palestine Exploration Fund began a new excavation at a major site near Gezer, Tell er-Rumeilah, the site of biblical Beth Shemesh. As their excavator the Fund hired Dr Duncan Mackenzie, who had worked at Helos for the British School of Archaeology at Athens, and assisted Sir Arthur Evans in excavations at Knossos in Crete, as well as carrying out what remains one of the most important prehistoric excavations in the Cyclades, at Phylakopi. As his assistant, Mr F. G. Newton, an architect, was appointed to make the plans and drawings. Mackenzie arrived in Jerusalem in July 1910, but, as the permit for excavation had not yet arrived, decided to make a tour of Moab and Edom with Mr Newton, in the course of which they made a number of interesting observations.

Excavations began in April 1911, on the western part of the tell. In the two seasons of work which he carried out at Beth Shemesh, Mackenzie was able to trace the line of the defences around the tell, and to clear the main gate of the town. The latest occupation of the site, on the south-east, was a Byzantine monastery. Outside the east wall of the town Mackenzie found a Late Bronze Age tomb containing imported Aegean pottery, which allowed cross-dating of the Levantine material. Although Macalister had been the first to use the 'Three Ages' terminology for the archaeological remains of the Holy Land in an unpublished letter to the Chairman of the Palestine Exploration Fund, Mackenzie became the first to use this terminology consistently and in its modern sense in his reporting of the results of his excavations at Beth Shemesh. Mackenzie's concept of stratigraphy was much more advanced than that of Macalister, and his recording system even included sections drawn to show the layers revealed in the profiles of his cuts. Mackenzie identified four strata, the earliest of which dated to the latter part of Late Bronze II, and ended with the cessation of the import of Mycenaean and Cypriote pottery. Stratum II was characterised by Philistine pottery, which Mackenzie was able to identify as such, and of which he was to provide the first adequate description, including linking it to the final Late Helladic (Mycenaean) pottery, thus showing the Aegean derivations of the Philistines for the first time. This stratum was destroyed by fire, the traces of which were discovered over the entire mound wherever this level was reached. Stratum III was an Israelite occupation, thought to end in 701 BC, with a destruction by Sennacherib, followed by an Israelite re-occupation in Stratum II. The final occupation, Stratum I, consisted of the Byzantine monastery. Later excavations revealed a few Neolithic and Chalcolithic items, but no permanent occupation, with the earliest occupation of the site falling in the Middle Bronze I culture.

Although this excavation did not produce the spectacular results of Macalister's work at Gezer, and has therefore often been disregarded, it was, in fact, a much better piece of work, and produced a number of significant advances in our understanding of the archaeology of the Holy Land.

The End of the Beginning: The Wilderness of Zin Survey

The final expedition, mounted before the outbreak of the First World War, was a curious one, but very fruitful. Late in 1912 Lord Kitchener, realising that war with Germany was inevitable, and that the Turks would probably come in on the side of the Germans, began to lay the plans for the conduct of the war in the Near East. His strategy was to attack the Turks from the south, sending an expeditionary force from Egypt through Palestine and Syria to move on the heartland of Turkey itself. The Geographical Section of the General Staff possessed good maps of all of the areas concerned except for the Sinai Peninsula and the Negev Desert south of the line of Wadi Beersheba. As the British were in control of Egypt, it was easy for the Royal Engineers to mount an expedition to map the Sinai, which was done, under the command of Captain S.F. Newcombe. For the Turkish side of the border things were more difficult, and some form of cover was needed. Kitchener suggested that the Palestine Exploration Fund be asked to provide this, and the Committee agreed. The Royal Engineers were to provide the surveying teams to make the map, and the Fund was to provide an archaeologist to carry out an archaeological survey, which would be published as fulfilling the ostensible purpose of the expedition. The archaeologist initially chosen was the Egyptologist, T.E.Peet; however, he turned out to have a prior engagement, and was unable to do the job. Sir Frederick Kenyon, director of the British Museum, was able to step in and provide two young archaeologists who were to be unemployed in the closed season of the excavations at Carchemish, when the Negev survey was to be carried out. Their names were Mr C.L.Woolley and Mr T.E.Lawrence.

Somewhat surprisingly, with hindsight, the Turks agreed to the proposal of the Fund, and work began in December 1913. The surveyors were divided into five parties, and set to work, completing the job by the end of May 1914, except for a small area near the head of the gulf of 'Aqaba, where the local governor made difficulties. Meanwhile, Woolley and Lawrence, sometimes travelling and working together and sometimes separately, visited the archaeological sites, planning, photographing, and making notes on the remains. They discovered the ruins of a number of large and prosperous Byzantine towns, extensive irrigation systems and reservoirs, temples, field systems, and dams. Their records of the towns of Esbeita, Abda/Oboda, Khalasa, ancient Elusa, and Kadesh Barnea still retain considerable value, especially so as some of the features which they recorded no longer exist. Before the results of the survey could be published, war had broken out, and both Woolley and Lawrence had been given commissions in the army, so their text was edited for publication by D.G.Hogarth. The volume included a sketch map drawn by B.V.Derbyshire, based on the survey map, which remained a military secret until it was finally published in 1921. As noted above, in spite of its exceedingly dubious origins, the archaeological results of this expedition were, and remain, of considerable value.

This was the last major archaeological expedition in the Holy Land before the First World War. After the war, in British Mandate Palestine, the situation was completely different. New figures emerged to take up the archaeological torch, perhaps most notably the distinguished American scholar, Dr, later Professor, William Foxwell Albright, who has been mentioned several times already. The postwar period, however, was no longer a period of pioneers, for the efforts of those past explorers, antiquaries and archaeologists, who, at considerable risk, sometimes at the cost of their lives, had laid a solid foundation for the modern study of the archaeology of the Holy Land. The outbreak of the war also marked the end of the period of British domination of the archaeology of the Holy Land. From the end of the First World War onwards there have been a multitude of expeditions from many countries, the United States, Canada, Britain, France, Germany, Australia, and even Japan. Additionally, since the Second World War the newly independent countries of the Middle East have produced their own distinguished archaeologists, who have taken their rightful place in the study of the past of their own homelands. Thus, today, the study of what has always been said to be a part of the heritage of all mankind is a truly international affair, to an extent which is hardly (if at all) equalled anywhere else in the world.

Suggestions for Further Reading

Drower, M.S.
  1985   *Flinders Petrie: A Life in Archaeology.* London: Victor Gollancz.
King, P.J.
  1983   *American Archaeology in the Mideast: A History of the American Schools of Oriental Research.* Philadelphia: The American Schools of Oriental Research.

Silberman, N.A.
  1982   *Digging for God and Country: Exploration, Archaeology, and the Secret Struggle for the Holy Land 1799–1917.* New York: Alfred A. Knopf.

Watson, Col. Sir C.M.
  1915   *Fifty Years' Work in the Holy Land: A Record and a Summary.* London: Palestine Exploration Fund.

Chapter 2
Geographical Background of the Holy Land
Peter G. Dorrell

The area we think of as the Holy Land covered the modern states of Israel and Jordan, although the frontiers within the region varied widely throughout history. The western boundary was always the Mediterranean, but although influences, and peoples, came from the sea, particularly from Cyprus and the Aegean, the inhabitants of the southern Levant did not turn to the Mediterranean, as the Phoenicians did. The eastern border was more indeterminate, sometimes lying along the Jordan river and sometimes further to the east where the trans-Jordan steppe gradually gives way to desert. In the south the Sinai desert formed an effective barrier to large-scale settlement, although not to communications: there were always trade and invasion routes along the sea coast in the south past Gaza. To the north the frontiers in the coastal area usually ran among the tangled and difficult hill country of southern Galilee, where the coastal plain narrows until it almost disappears south of Tyre. On the other side of the Jordan Valley, however, the northern approach is much more open, constricted only by the basalt country of the Jebel Druze, which in earlier times confined movement to a broad corridor east of the Great Rift Valley. Here the frontiers of antiquity moved north and south according to the relative strengths of the local kingdoms, moving even more as the great powers to the north and east (Babylon, Assyria, Persia and the Hittites) and the great power to the south (Egypt) were in ascendancy or decline.

Longitudinally the land is divided into four zones by topography and climate, and consequently by the soils and vegetation and the opportunities for settlement. (A map showing geographical features appears on page 8.)

The most westerly strip, the coastal plain, is broad in the south and narrows to the north, broken by the bold headland of Mt Carmel. In the south there are wide areas of dunes and drifting sands. Farther north are long ridges of hard consolidated sand dunes which in antiquity created lagoons and swamps, forming a barrier between the coast and the hinterland and pushing the main north-south routeway inland. There are many short, steep streams which drain the high ground towards the east. In the south most are only seasonal, becoming fierce, erosive torrents in winter and after rain in the hills, but drying up completely in summer. The Mt Carmel ridge runs south-east to north-west, cutting across the grain of the country. This steep-sided fold of limestone shelters to the north the bay of Acco, one of the few anchorages along the coast, and the valley of Jezreel which cuts through the highlands and broadens to the plain of Beth Shan, joining the Jordan Valley. The great coastal road – one of the major routes of the ancient world – crossed the ridge of Carmel by the pass of Megiddo, and the Jordan Valley between Lake Huleh and Lake Tiberias, and continued on to Damascus and the north. The coastal plain was never very productive in antiquity, but drainage and irrigation have made it intensely fertile in recent times.

Behind the coastal plain, foothills rise to the central ridge of the country. These foothills – the Shephela – were wooded in antiquity and heavily settled, particularly in several alluvial valleys. These slopes, and the higher ground above, supported the classic trinity of Mediterranean tillage; wheat, olives and vines. Between them and the higher and rockier land to the east lies a valley or trench of softer and more easily eroded limestone, which provided a line of demarcation and defence through much of biblical times. The summit-line of the ridge, along which stood many important towns of Iron Age and Bronze Age times – Beersheba, Hebron, Jerusalem and Shechem – marks the watershed between the western-flowing streams draining to the Mediterranean and the very few intermittent wadis flowing eastward to the Great Rift Valley. East of the summit-line the hills are rainless for much of the year and have always been suitable for seasonal grazing and very little else, a barren wilderness which plunges steeply down to the central divide of the Jordan Valley.

The valley itself, the third of the longitudinal divisions of the country, is part of the major structural rift running up from east Africa to form the Red Sea, the Dead Sea, the Jordan Valley, Lake Tiberias, and Lake Huleh. Farther north a similar, although geologically distinct, trench swings slightly eastward from the north–south alignment and forms the Beq'a, the valley between the Lebanon and Antilebanon mountains. North of this valley again the coastal mountains continue almost without interruption to join the highlands of Anatolia, while the inland range separates and spreads out to the north-east as a series of fan-like ridges at a lower elevation. This basic structural division of the Levant not only governs the physical geography of all the countries along the coast but is a major influence on the weather pattern, and on vegetation, agriculture, settlement and means of communication.

In the southern Levant the trench has always presented a considerable obstacle to east–west movement. On both sides the slopes are precipitous, with only a few easy ways through. South of the Dead Sea is the wide, almost waterless Wadi Arabah. North of the Dead Sea – the lowest body of water on earth – the valley narrows to a few kilometres, but the River Jordan itself presents a considerable obstacle, deeply entrenched in a ribbon of dense riverine forest, and flanked along much of its course by dissected badlands of marl. There are few crossing-points south of Lake Tiberias. The centre of the valley never attracted settlement, particularly since the soils were, and are, heavily saline. On the eastern side of the valley there were ancient settlements, where hillside streams flow out into the valley floor, but on the western side the lack of streams and the low rainfall caused by the rain-shadow effects of the hills limited settlement to a few oases such as Jericho, and to the lower end of the side valley of Beth Shan.

East of the Jordan Valley lies the almost continuous scarp-front of the Jordan highlands, the fourth zone. The hills are high and rugged in the south, formed from ancient granites and sandstones (the well-known Nubian sandstone in which the façades of Petra are cut). East of the Dead Sea the hills flatten down to a high plateau of rolling steppe country, become higher and more folded in Gilead, north of Amman, and then lose height again in the open uplands of Bashan. This area, Bashan and the Hauran, was known in antiquity as one of the great granaries of the region, and it was equally well known for its cattle. The Gilead was famous for vines, and in the sheltered valleys for olives. Farther south was pastureland, although cereals also flourished in southern Moab and Edom, where the greater height of the hills lay in the path of western, rain-bearing winds.

Beyond the crest-line of the ridge, the land slopes gently down to the east, becoming more arid and less fertile towards the desert interior. Only seasonal wadis drain the slope, most of which are lost in the Wadi Sirhan, the great shallow depression which runs south-east into Arabia.

The weather pattern of the Levant coastal lands is typically Mediterranean: rain is confined to a few winter months, with short sharp downpours between days of clear skies, rather than the longer-lasting depressions of more northerly latitudes. The summer is settled, and is normally without rain between April and October. Most of the rain comes from onshore depressions originating in the eastern Mediterranean (although there are occasional incursions of colder, drier air from the north-west and north-east). Thus the coastal plain, the foothills, and the western ridge are well-watered, while rainfall totals fall off abruptly in the Jordan Valley (the area around the Dead Sea receives no more than 50 mm per annum) and rise again on the higher parts of the eastern plateau, finally dying away eastward into the dry steppes and desert. In addition to this west-to-east gradient, the rainfall diminishes quite abruptly from north to south, so that south of Gaza the desert reaches almost to the sea-coast. Where the western ridge is lower, rain-bearing winds penetrate farther to the east, giving eastward extensions of the band of arable land across the Jordan. This occurs opposite the Low Negev, the Jezreel Valley, and, farther north opposite the Homs-Palmyra gap in Syria, and again behind the Syrian Saddle, the low pass at the extreme north-east corner of the Mediterranean.

As well as being lower in total towards the east, the rainfall also becomes less reliable, with greater inter-annual variability. Wide areas of steppe are therefore marginal – available for pastoral use, where flocks can move to take advantage of different areas of rainfall, but, in antiquity at least, not open to regular cultivation. Annual rainfall totals vary from 7–500 mm on the higher ground in the north to 100 mm or less in the extreme south and east. But these general totals mask considerable local variations due to local topography and aspect. Moreover, the climate has fluctuated over time, though the general distribution probably remained much the same.

Temperatures follow roughly the same pattern, higher in the south and east, but again there are many local anomalies: snow is common, though rarely long-lying, in the mountains, with less in the foothills, and uncommon in the coastal plain. In the Jordan Valley it is virtually unknown, and frost is very rare. It snows occasionally in the northern parts of the trans-Jordan hills, especially in Gilead, but less often than in the west. Temperatures in summer can be very high, particularly in the Jordan valley and in other parts of the region that are not open to the tempering effects of onshore breezes. Occasional incursions of hot, dry desert winds from the south and south-east can have a serious effect on vegetation, especially in spring when field crops can be badly parched.

Overall, then, the land is of great diversity. The shape of the country itself, with its strong north–south divisions; the pattern of the weather, partly global but greatly influenced by local topography; and the position of the area, at the confined junction of the great land masses of Europe, Asia and Africa: all these have contributed to its character as a meeting place and a crossing point. Within very short distances there are many different types of country, of vegetation, soils and climate, and different opportunities for settlement and agriculture. Because of its position, throughout history, it has been open to cultural and social influences from nearly all points of the compass. Armies have marched through it and fought over it; different cultures, religions and languages have been introduced or have developed in one or other of its regions. Perhaps this very openness, this vulnerability to so many pressures, is responsible for its stubborn sense of identity and character.

Chapter 3
Biblical Archaeology: A Synthesis and Overview
Jonathan N. Tubb

The results of more than a hundred years of active fieldwork and research in the Holy Land cannot adequately be described in these few pages, and the following is merely an attempt to provide a sort of cultural canvas upon which can be painted the events so wonderfully and richly described in the Bible. Archaeology, in providing this framework, has made an invaluable contribution to our understanding and appreciation of the biblical stories, and indeed one which offers a new perspective from which the narratives can be viewed.

It is difficult in a brief review of this nature to know exactly where to begin. From the point of view that this book is concerned more with biblical archaeology than with Palestinian archaeology in the broader sense, it would seem inappropriate to discuss at length the periods of remote prehistory. On the other hand the biblical 'core period' cannot be examined in isolation without some reference to its ancestry, and therefore, in order to accommodate both of these considerations, a rather arbitrary decision has been taken to begin the discussion with the Neolithic period of the eighth millennium BC.

Prehistory: The Neolithic and Chalcolithic Periods

Much of our knowledge concerning the early prehistory of Palestine comes from the work undertaken at the site of Jericho in southern Palestine. Here excavations conducted by Dame Kathleen Kenyon, on behalf of the British School of Archaeology in Jerusalem between 1952 and 1958, revealed a remarkable sequence of occupation phases belonging to the Neolithic period (8000–4500 BC). In fact settlement at the site predates the Neolithic. Evidence was found for what seems to have been a type of sanctuary, constructed near the Spring of 'Ain es-Sultan by the Natufian hunter-gatherers of the Mesolithic period. It was undoubtedly due to the presence of this perennial spring that some of these Mesolithic hunters, or their descendants, decided to settle permanently on the site. Initially they built themselves light and insubstantial shelters (leaving little in the archaeological record except for patterns of post-holes), but these were eventually replaced by more permanent structures built of mud-brick. At Jericho, perhaps as early as the tenth millennium BC, can be witnessed, therefore, the vital transition from nomadism to sedentism and indeed also, the accompanying processes of plant and animal domestication which define the so-called 'neolithic revolution'. This fundamental socio-economic change did not, of course, happen overnight and may have taken anything up to a thousand years. Certainly by about 7000 BC Jericho had developed into a very substantial

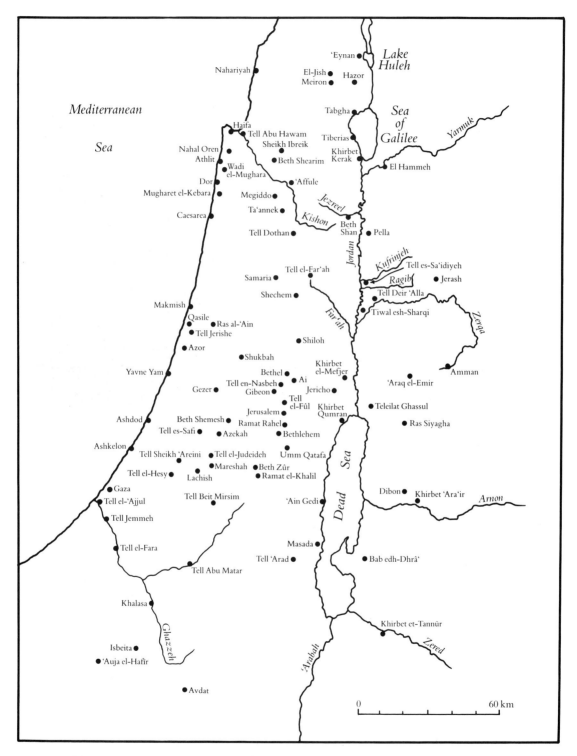

Map of the Levant showing principal excavated sites.

9. Tell es-Sultan, ancient Jericho, from the west. (photo: PGD)

settlement. Indeed, even within the context of its milieu, Jericho must be seen as something of an anomaly. For although several settlements of this pre-pottery phase of the neolithic (known as Pre-Pottery Neolithic A) are known throughout the Levant, most were no more than small un-walled villages. Jericho, on the other hand, can truly be described as a town with massive defensive walls and at least one impressively constructed stone-built tower. The Pre-Pottery Neolithic A people lived in well-built mud-brick houses which were circular or oval in plan. As far as the economy was concerned, there were still no domestic animals and the chief source of meat was gazelle, either herded or hunted. With regard to plant domestication, however, a major breakthrough had occurred with the domestication of two-row hulled barley and emmer wheat.

At Jericho, as elsewhere in the Levant, the Pre-Pottery Neolithic A culture was succeeded by the Pre-Pottery Neolithic B. Although some degree of continuity is recognised between these two phases, changes in the material culture suggest the introduction of new peoples, perhaps from the north. The settlement which may have contained as many as 2000 individuals was again defended by a substantial wall, but the houses were of a new design, being rectilinear rather than circular. Most were provided with finely laid lime-plaster floors often stained red, orange or pink and polished smooth.

The dead were often buried below the floors of houses and although most of the burials are unremarkable, the corpses having simply been placed in a loosely contracted position without grave goods, some are quite extraordinary. For in many instances the skull had been removed, and had then been carefully and sensitively remodelled with plaster to build up the facial features. Shells, either bivalves or cowries, were then set into the empty sockets to represent the eyes. These plastered skulls were further decorated with red and black paint to depict individual characteristics such as hair and even moustaches. The Jericho plastered skulls have often been cited as evidence of an ancestor cult, and this is certainly reasonable, but their value is perhaps even greater in reflecting a highly sophisticated and technically accomplished artistic tradition. In this respect Jericho does not stand alone. The Pre-Pottery Neolithic B culture was widespread throughout the Levant and indeed similarly plastered skulls have been found at sites in Palestine, Syria and Jordan. At Tell Ramad in Syria, plaster and clay female figures have been

10. (*left*) Pre-Pottery Neolithic A tower at Jericho. (photo: PGD)

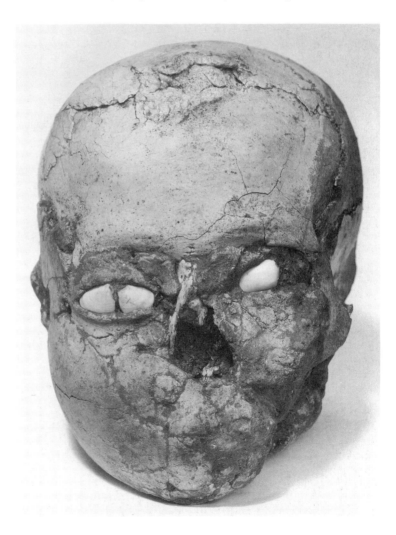

11. (*right*) Pre-Pottery Neolithic B plastered skull from Jericho. (BM WA 127414)

45

found which are thought to have served as supports for the plastered skulls. Other aspects of Pre-Pottery Neolithic B artistic and craft skills have recently been demonstrated by discoveries at Nahal Hemar, a cave site in the Judean desert near the southern end of the Dead Sea. Here exceptional environmental conditions within the cave allowed for the preservation of a wide range of organic materials, which in normal archaeological contexts would not have survived.

Skulls were again found at Nahal Hemar, although here they were not plastered, but instead were covered with asphalt, modelled in a lattice pattern over the top and back to represent hair. Also found were human figurines of carved bone decorated with asphalt and coloured pigments, stone masks, beads made of shells and painted wood and a variety of baskets and finely woven textiles.

Undoubtedly the most remarkable discovery of recent years, however, was made in 1983 at the Neolithic site of 'Ain Ghazal on the outskirts of Amman in Jordan. Here, buried in a pit which had been dug into the floor of an abandoned house dating to the Pre-Pottery Neolithic B period, was found a cache of extraordinary statues, modelled in lime plaster over armatures of reeds and twine. The statues fall into two categories according to their size: the smaller, approximately 35 cm in height, are referred to as 'dumpies' and the larger, approximately 90 cm in height, are termed 'figures'. In both cases heads and faces are naturalistically rendered, but whereas the dumpies have only schematised bodies or perhaps busts, the figures have realistically represented bodies with arms and legs, feet and hands, and in some cases breasts. Many of the 'Ain Ghazal statues were decorated with paint or with shallow incision to indicate hair, items of clothing and also to highlight the facial features. Most striking of all, however, is the treatment of the eyes which were built up in a purer whiter plaster than was used for the main statues. A black bituminous material was used to create the iris-pupils and the same material was pressed into grooves surrounding the eyeballs, but here the effect was further enhanced by the addition of an unusual green mineral pigment, dioptase.

Both Neolithic cultures described above flourished during a period prior to the invention of pottery, and whilst an interesting material known as 'white ware' composed of lime and salty grey ashes was used to produce simple vessels at Pre-Pottery Neolithic B sites in Syria, true pottery did not appear in the Levant until the sixth millennium BC.

The Pottery Neolithic did not follow the Pre-Pottery Neolithic B directly, however. At Jericho, as elsewhere in the Levant, there seems to have been a gap in occupation lasting for some 500 years. Most plausibly this discontinuity can be related to the onset of drier climatic conditions which would have caused a major disruption to the early Neolithic economy. When permanent settlement did return to the country towards the middle of the sixth millennium, it was on a much poorer scale. Certainly Jericho was no longer a strongly defended thriving town, but instead had reverted to being a simple unwalled village. The pattern in the rest of the country was much the same and until approximately the middle of the fifth millennium, Palestine witnessed a complicated series of partly successive, partly contemporaneous, village-based cultures, distinguished from one another by differences in their pottery styles.

The number of settlements in Palestine and Transjordan increased greatly during the period from the mid-fifth millennium to the end of the fourth millennium, that is in the period known as the Chalcolithic. The main characteristics of this interesting phase were first defined on the basis of the excavations conducted at the site of Teleilat Ghassul, situated east of the River Jordan and close to the northern end of the Dead Sea. Ghassul was a large open settlement, covering some 60 acres and was composed of well-constructed rectangular mud–brick houses. In addition to purely domestic housing, the settlement had two cultic centres, contained within a walled enclosure.

A further dimension to the Chalcolithic culture of Palestine has been provided by more recent research in the vicinity of Beersheba and in the hills to the west of the Dead Sea. Chronologically the settlements of these regions overlap with Ghassul, beginning and ending slightly later, but nevertheless it has now become customary to discuss the Chalcolithic period in terms of the Ghassul-Beersheba culture. At Beersheba rectangular

12. Pre-Pottery Neolithic B lime plaster statues from 'Ain Ghazal. (photo: KWT)

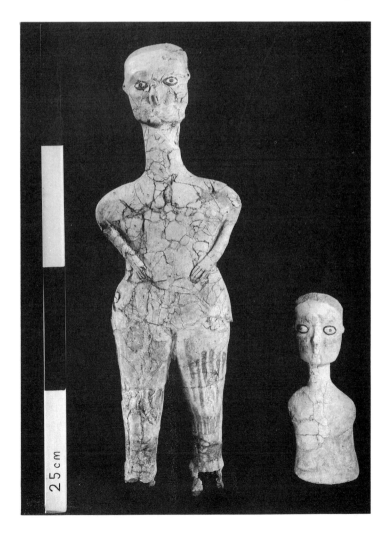

houses, similar to those at Ghassul, have been found, but in the initial phases of settlement some of the population, at least, appear to have lived in troglodyte dwellings.

The term 'Chalcolithic' is of course derived from the Greek word for copper and evidence has been found in many regions for an active and sophisticated metal industry in this period. In Sinai and the Negev many settlements or camps have been found associated with the mining and production of copper (and also turquoise), and at Abu Matar, one of the Beersheba sites, considerable evidence for metalworking has been found in the form of raw malachite, flint anvils for ore crushing, ovens and crucibles. That the copper industry was advanced and sophisticated is clear from the extraordinary hoard of copper objects found in the cave of Nahal Mishmar in the hills to the west of the Dead Sea. The hoard contained highly decorative objects, for the most part probably ritual in function, such as mace heads, wands and crown-like objects which may have fitted together to form altars.

The Nahal Mishmar hoard highlights another important aspect of the Chalcolithic period: its highly developed artistic traditions. At Ghassul remarkable wall-paintings were found, showing elaborate geometric designs, face-masks and human figures. The Beersheba sites produced highly accomplished ivory carving including male and female figures in the round, and unusual sickles decorated by incisions. Bone and ivory were also used in the making of plaques with openwork or incised ornament, the design produced by a series of small perforations filled with bitumen.

In the coastal region of Palestine, principally in the Tel Aviv area, a series of artificial caves have been found cut into the rock, and inside these, arranged along benches and on the floors, were numbers of burial chests or ossuaries. Some of these were made

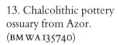

13. Chalcolithic pottery ossuary from Azor. (BM WA 135740)

of stone, but the majority were of pottery, and the most interesting appear to represent houses with pitched roofs, exposed beams, doors and little rectangular windows.

It is not clear as to exactly what happened to the Ghassul-Beersheba culture towards the end of the fourth millennium BC; it seems simply to have died out. Certainly this interesting and artistically imaginative culture does not appear to have made a major contribution to the subsequent Early Bronze Age culture of the third millennium BC.

The Early Bronze Age and the Rise of Urbanism

By the end of the fourth millennium BC literate and urban civilisations had been established in Egypt, Syria and Mesopotamia and the consequent opening of a complex system of trade routes produced the stimulus for a similar development in Palestine, albeit on a smaller scale. Many of the small village settlements of the Chalcolithic period were abandoned and new groups of people entering the country around 3200 BC established themselves at new sites deliberately selected for their natural resources, and designed to benefit from the expanding web of trade connections. In many instances sites were founded which were destined to become major centres for the following three millennia, and for this reason this period, which stands at the very threshold of the Early Bronze Age, is often referred as the Proto-Urban.

The transition to the Early Bronze Age proper at the start of the third millennium BC was marked, or more properly was determined, by a fundamental change in the country's economic basis. For, in order for Palestine to play a role in the international trading community of the third millennium, the old village-based economy of subsistence dry-farming and pastoralism had to give way to one of productive agriculture leading to trade. This change generated in itself a spiral of demographic and socio-economic processes linked directly with the growth of urbanism. For the new economy required organisation, administration and of course manpower. With expansion came social differentiation and the development of an appropriate bureaucratic infrastructure required to initiate and oversee the necessary public building programmes. Irrigation too, essential for effective agriculture and horticulture, required organisation and labour. Water supply was of prime concern, not only for irrigation, but on a domestic level for sustaining the growing population. It is hardly accidental that the majority of Early Bronze Age settlements were established close to perennial rivers or streams. Where the supply was inadequate, quite elaborate provision was made for the catchment and storage of run-off water. At Arad, for example, a large artificial reservoir was constructed in order to collect run-off rainwater.

The Early Bronze Age saw the development of strong and effective defensive systems. At Arad, one of the best preserved and most extensively excavated sites, the settlement was protected by a substantial stone-built wall, provided at regular intervals with semi-circular bastions. At Jericho the town wall was built of mud-brick on stone foundations and was initially 1 m thick. By the end of the period the width had increased to a substantial 5 metres, and the wall, like Arad, was protected by bastions, in this case square in plan. Some of the Early Bronze Age defensive systems were extremely elaborate, and in their design concept clearly anticipate the so-called 'Hyksos' fortifications of the Middle Bronze Age. At Tell Ta'anek, for example, the final phase of the Early Bronze Age defences consisted of two parallel walls with a passageway between. Against the outer wall was placed a massive sloping fill held in place at the base by a third revetment wall.

Within the town walls Early Bronze Ages sites generally show well-constructed houses built either of stone or mud-brick on stone foundations. That some form of town planning was in operation is evident from the results of excavations at a number of sites. At Tell es-Sa'idiyeh in the Jordan Valley the Early Bronze Age settlement was laid out on a regularly orientated grid of intersecting streets, and similar grid patterns have been found at Megiddo and Tell el-Far'ah (north). At Arad, where a large exposure of the Early Bronze Age settlement has been made, the insulae of housing units were separated from a precinct of public buildings, including a 'palace', administrative buildings and a pair of temples.

14. Early Bronze II pottery vessels including 'Abydos' jug and juglets from Tell es-Sa'idiyeh. (BM WA collections)

The material culture of Palestine during the Early Bronze Age displays a high level of technical accomplishment. The pottery repertoire is characterised by simplicity and elegance, particularly evident in the series of graceful jugs and juglets. The range of forms also includes bowls, cups, platters, jars of various shapes and sizes, and cooking pots. The effects of urbanism can clearly be seen in the diversification of the repertoire with differentiation into utilitarian and storage wares, table wares and funerary wares (often miniature vessels). Many of the vessels were decorated with a highly burnished red or brownish-purple slip and others show varieties of painted designs. Technically the pottery of the Early Bronze Age is far superior to that of the preceding periods: clays were well prepared, the wheel was commonly used and the firing was carefully controlled. Similar advances in metal technology can also be observed. Although relatively little Early Bronze Age metalwork has survived, the majority having presumably been melted down and re-used in antiquity, examples of tools and weapons that have been analysed show a good understanding of the principles of alloying (although not yet with tin to produce true bronzes) and methods of casting.

Palestine's rise to full urbanism during the Early Bronze Age had yet another consequence manifested in the burial customs. For permanence of settlement over several generations led to the practice of multiple successive burial in what may be seen as family tombs. The tombs were generally rock-cut, with a well-excavated subterranean chamber entered by means of a vertical shaft. Burials were placed inside the tomb, successively over a long period of time. As each new interment was made, the remains of the previous deceased were rather unceremoniously swept to the sides of the tomb. The skulls only, having been neatly detached from the bodies, were accorded some respect and were carefully arranged around the walls. The process was repeated over many generations so that at Jericho, for example, several of the tombs contained well over 100 individuals. Grave goods were placed inside the tombs. For the most part these consisted of pottery vessels, many undoubtedly containing food and drink for the afterlife. Others were less purely functional: an interesting series of miniature vessels suggests that aesthetic considerations were also of importance.

In the absence of directly relevant written records, the political situation in Palestine during the Early Bronze Age is difficult to reconstruct. It is often suggested that the country was composed of independent city states, each controlling an area in its immediate vicinity which would have included a number of dependent villages. This model seems very plausible, although 'city-state' is perhaps too grand a term to describe what were in reality little more than market towns, certainly when compared with sites in Meso-potamia or Syria. There is no evidence to suggest that any one town exercised political hegemony, but it is possible that there was a shifting balance of political power throughout the period, with one town gaining for a limited time a certain supremacy over its neigh-bours, to be replaced later by another and so on.

It is certainly clear that it was not a particularly peaceful period. Judging from the number of times the defences of any one town were destroyed and repaired, the Early Bronze Age must have seen almost continuous strife. At Jericho, for example, the defences

15. Tell ed-Duweir, ancient Lachish, from the north-east. The site was extensively occupied during the Early Bronze Age. (photo: BM/WT)

at certain points are reckoned to have been repaired some seventeen times. Most of the conflict was probably on a local level, towns involved in territorial disputes or inter-necine feuds. There is however evidence to suggest that relations with Egypt were not always on a strictly commercial basis. An Egyptian wall-painting from a tomb at Deshasheh shows the Egyptian attack on a Palestinian town. Interestingly, the town is represented as being surrounded by a strong defensive wall with semi-circular bastions at regular intervals – exactly the type of fortification system found by excavation at Arad. Whilst Egyptian campaigns were undoubtedly launched from time to time against Palestinian towns, especially those in the south of the country, there is no evidence to suggest that Egypt exercised any form of political control. Egyptian objects, mostly luxury goods such as stone palettes and stone vessels, found at Palestinian sites represent items of trade and do not imply a political presence. Indeed, these objects would be expected to occur in some number since, beyond any question, Egypt formed the main market for Palestine's produce. Commodities such as wine and olive oil were in great demand, and it is significant to note that a particular form of Palestinian jug, eminently suitable for the transport and storage of such goods, has been found in many of the Egyptian Royal tombs of the First Dynasty at Abydos. In fact so common was this type of vessel, that despite its undisputed Palestinian manufacture, it has become known as the ''Abydos jug'. Much of the trade was by sea, and in this respect the port of Byblos on the Lebanese coast was of key importance. Almost more than any other material, the Egyptians required timber; with access to the hinterland of the Lebanese forests, Byblos became the major exporter, and enjoyed for much of its history a particularly close relationship with Egypt.

Overland trade was probably conducted by means of donkey caravans. At Lachish the bones of a domesticated ass were found in a tomb of the Early Bronze Age. Trading relations were not exclusively with Egypt and sites in the north of the country, such as Hazor or Megiddo, undoubtedly formed links with central and north Syria. Recent discoveries at Tell Mardikh, ancient Ebla, south of Aleppo, have revealed, during the Early Bronze Age, a thriving and highly sophisticated Syrian culture. The finding there of a major archive of clay tablets has added a new dimension to our understanding of the international relations in the third millennium BC. For, although relatively few of the texts have been translated so far, it is clear that by about 2500 BC Ebla exercised some form of political control as far south as Damascus, and had commercial ties over an even wider area. This would help to explain the increasing number of Syrian objects found at sites in the north of Palestine, which must now be taken as evidence for the establishment of active commercial relations between the two regions.

Economic Recession: The Early Bronze IV Interlude

Conventionally the Early Bronze Age has been divided into four main phases, distinguished from one another largely on the basis of changes in pottery styles. The foregoing discussion has been concerned with the first three of these, from the formative Early Bronze I to the full flowering of the culture in Early Bronze II–III (2850–2400 BC). Characterisation and understanding of the fourth phase, Early Bronze IV (2400–2000), has eluded scholars for nearly a century, and only comparatively recently has a consensus been reached which allows this enigmatic phase to be seen as a logical continuation of the culture of EB II–III. For so pronounced are the changes apparent in the material culture, settlement pattern and economy of EB IV that many scholars believed that they could only be explained in terms of a complete culture break, resulting from widespread destructions of EB III towns and involving mass invasions of nomadic barbarians. Arguments were advanced which had waves of Amorites, and at times even the biblical patriarchs, pouring into Palestine during the last quarter of the third millennium BC.

Most recent analyses of the EB IV period have tended to minimise or eliminate such theories, which depend upon dubious or inappropriate linguistic evidence, and involve ethnic movements. Instead it is now possible to explain the characteristics of the period as localised and regional responses to changes in the economic situation and as relating also to the processes of urbanism.

For, as we have seen, the rise to urbanism of Palestine during the Early Bronze Age can be related directly to the establishment of extensive commercial relations principally (certainly in central and southern parts of the country) with Egypt. Towards the end of the third millennium, the Old Kingdom in Egypt faltered and then collapsed, leading to a total cessation of trade links. The economic basis of Early Bronze Age Palestine, which had been dependent upon this commercial relationship, was therefore swept away. The effects, as might be expected, were profound. The loss of the Egyptian markets meant effectively that the economy, which had been geared towards productive agriculture and trade, was no longer appropriate, and as a consequence urban settlement could no longer be sustained.

The effects were most severe in central and southern Palestine, where nearly every site has produced evidence for either abandonment or settlement on a vastly diminished scale. The population appears either to have moved to areas such as Transjordan or the Negev where a living could be made out of subsistence dry-farming, or to have adopted a semi-sedentary seasonal occupation related most probably to pastoralism. In Palestine, in the absence of settlement sites, most of our information concerning the EB IV period has come from tombs, of which very many have been excavated. Large cemeteries have been found, many at established settlement sites of the EB II–III periods, such as Jericho and Lachish, and whilst the fashion for shaft tombs, often with quite large chambers, continued, interesting changes in the burial practices can be observed. For in contrast with the tombs of the earlier phases of the Early Bronze Age, which

16. Processing the pottery at Lachish in the 1930s. Seated at the bench is Gerald Lankester Harding, who later became Director General of Antiquities of Jordan. Climbing the steps is Olga Tufnell, who completed publication of the results following the tragic death of the expedition's director, J.L.Starkey, in 1938. The shelves contain many Early Bronze IV vessels from the site's extensive cemeteries of that period. (photo: BM/WT)

17. Tiwal esh-Sharqi, an Early Bronze Age cemetery site excavated by the writer in 1984. In the foreground is the Wadi Zerqa. (photo: PGD)

tended to contain multiple successive burials, those of the EB IV period generally contain only one interment. Furthermore, the burials are most commonly seen to be secondary: that is, the bodies were allowed to decompose before the bones were collected up for deposition in the tomb. Both of these features can be directly related to the changes in the socio-economic and geo-locational situation. Lack of habitual permanent settlement would rule against multiple successive burials, and the secondary burial practice might well result from the process of periodic returns of the deceased to traditionally established burial grounds. Certainly in Transjordan, an area in which refugees of the economic recession appear to have settled, the burial customs are seen to be somewhat different and continue more clearly those of the preceding period. In 1984 the writer conducted a season of excavations at the site of Tiwal esh-Sharqi, an EB IV cemetery on the south bank of the Zarqa, close to the Jordan river. The cemetery served the occupation site of Tell Umm-Hammad, which, during the period in question, appears to have been an extensive and permanent settlement approaching the status of a town. Over forty tombs were excavated, mostly of the shaft tomb variety, and here, undoubtedly due to the permanent settlement, many of the tombs contained double or multiple interments. In addition, in only one case was evidence found for a secondary practice, this otherwise being clearly inappropriate for the situation of a settlement immediately adjacent to its cemetery.

Not only in the realm of burial practices does the EB IV culture differ markedly from that of EB II–III. The fundamental change in the life-style resulting from the collapse of the Early Bronze Age economy produced equally radical, yet again fully understandable changes in the material culture. The pottery traditions of the period, irrespective of regionally individualistic traits, reflected the needs of the communities by rejecting the elaborate and delicate luxury vessels, replacing them instead with more functional and multi-purpose pieces. The effect was to produce a somewhat restricted repertoire, yet one which was suited to a period of undoubted austerity. The change in the economy can also be seen as responsible for the disappearance of the commercial store-jar: there was simply no market for bulk commodities. Yet it would be a mistake to see these

18. Typical shaft tomb at Tiwal esh-Sharqi, showing the entrance to the chamber and its stone blocking. (photo: PGD)

19. Early Bronze IV pottery vessels from various tombs at Tiwal esh-Sharqi. (BM WA collections)

changes as evidence for decline or regression. For, superimposed upon what may be described as the 'rationalisation' of the pottery traditions, were technological advances involving, for example, the more extensive use of the fast wheel. The advances are again more apparent at sites which show more extensive and more permanent occupation. The pottery of Tiwal esh-Sharqi, for example, was superbly made: the clays well prepared, the firing even and carefully controlled and the skilful use of the fast wheel producing wonderfully thin-walled vessels.

Early Bronze IV metalwork also, whilst perhaps more closely reflecting the typological continuity of EB II–III traditions, shows similar technological advances. Improved casting techniques were responsible for one of the most characteristic EB IV weapon types, the so-called 'fenestrated' or 'eye' axe and by the middle of the period deliberate alloying with tin produced the first true bronzes.

As stated earlier, the collapse of the Egyptian Old Kingdom had its most severe effects in the southern and central parts of Palestine. The situation in the north of the country may have been slightly different. The factors contributing to the decline of urban life may well have been less sharply felt, delayed in their effects or offset by compensatory factors. In the absence of Egypt as a commercial market it is probable that the northern towns still maintained, if not increased, trading activities with inland Syria which, during the whole of this period, boasted a flourishing and highly sophisticated civilisation. Indeed, such commercial ties are hinted at in the economic texts from the archives of Tell Mardikh, ancient Ebla just south of Aleppo, and more tangible evidence comes from the quite large numbers of imported Syrian 'caliciform' wares, painted teapots and goblets found for example at Hazor, Megiddo and Beth Shan.

Given these circumstances, it is quite likely that instead of a total shift in population from urban to non-urban situation, the north of the country witnessed what may fairly be described as a period of severe recession, and most probably one which was shorter than the EB IV period elsewhere. At Megiddo, for example, there is some evidence for continuation of settlement, although on a much diminished scale. Not only did one of its temples continue in use, but at some stage the site was provided with weak fortifications. Tombs with multiple burials were also found at Megiddo, again arguing for a greater degree of settlement.

Revival: The Beginning of the Middle Bronze Age

The foregoing discussion makes it clear that the Early Bronze IV period in Palestine must be seen as an interlude – a temporary set-back in the inevitable developmental process which brought the country to fully urban civilisation. Despite the many internal complexities which still require elucidation, the distinctive culture must be explained in terms of an indigenously based alteration in life-style in response to changed economic circumstances. It is important also to appreciate that the conventionally agreed chronological division of the Early Bronze Age fails to take into account the really quite complex socio-culture interfaces which undoubtedly occurred for variable durations and in variable manifestations throughout the country. In other words, EB IV did not follow EB III in any strictly chronological sense, but rather it is possible to conceive of EB IV cultural attributes being present, to some degree, in some elements of society from at least the end of EB II, Such a rationalisation is necessary, for the economic failure of Egypt, itself not a sudden event, could not have had an immediate unilateral effect on the towns of Palestine. Instead it had established an uneasy equilibrium – a balance between urbanism and agriculture on the one hand and semi-sedentism and pastoralism on the other. The balance of the dimorphic society which this process generated was largely determined by externally imposed variables. At the beginning of the period of recession the EB II–III element was dominant, but as the recession gripped the country ever harder, the EB IV element achieved superiority. Taking these considerations into account, there would seem to be very little reason to suggest an external origin for the Middle Bronze Age culture which followed. For the reversion to urbanism, which occurred during this period, should be seen as precisely that, made possible by the reversal of those factors which had contributed to the demise of the urban communities of the Early Bronze Age.

In Egypt political and economic stability was restored towards the end of the third millennium BC by the unification of the country under Mentuhotpe II, the founder of the Middle Kingdom. Under his vigorous and energetic rule, the administration was again centralised and the trade routes re-opened. Conditions were therefore re-established which favoured a return to urbanism in Palestine, with a corresponding shift in the economic basis. Again the processes of this quite gradual change were extremely complex and are perhaps largely intangible with regard to the archaeological record. Only the material culture bears witness to the outcome of the change in the socio-economic situation: the Middle Bronze Age culture which emerged should be seen not only as reflecting the shift of the equilibrium in favour of urbanism, but also as being a revitalisation of inherent ideals preserved throughout a period during which an urban mode of existence was simply not possible. It is not surprising, therefore, that the material culture of the Middle Bronze Age, especially in its initial phase (the MB IIA), combines elements transmitted directly through the EB IV interlude with others which, mainly through reasons of inappropriateness, had lain dormant since the EB II and III periods. This is clearest perhaps in the pottery. The vessels of the early part of the Middle Bronze Age are arguably the most aesthetically beautiful ever produced in Palestine, combining as they do technologically advanced production methods, which had been developed during the course of the EB IV, with a formal elegance, the inspiration for which can be traced back to the EB II and III. The return to urban life provided once again a demand for luxury and table wares, allowing the Middle Bronze Age potter to expand his repertoire to include a wide range of graceful jugs, juglets and pitchers as well as wonderfully fine-walled carinated bowls, developed perhaps from metal prototypes. The re-establishment of the trade routes necessitated the return of the commercial store-jar to the repertoire, now clearly designed with transport in mind.

The return of Palestine to full urbanism in the Middle Bronze Age is also reflected in the burial customs. The re-establishment of permanent communities led to the gradual re-introduction of the traditional practice of multiple successive primary burial. The rock-cut shaft tomb was still the favoured type of tomb and in many instances the somewhat sparsely occupied EB IV tombs were re-used. Also found in the earliest phase of the Middle Bronze Age (the MB IIA), however, is a completely different type of burial. Several sites have produced small numbers of stone-lined graves, rectangular or sub-rectangular in shape and covered normally with large limestone slabs. The grave goods accompanying the deceased in the stone-lined graves are generally seen to be richer or more elaborate than those of the contemporary shaft tombs, including, for example, finely decorated pottery vessels or rich assemblages of metal weapons, and it would not be unreasonable to suggest that these were the graves of certain persons of elevated social status. So different in concept are the stone-lined graves from the traditional shaft tombs that it might be argued that they represent the burials of an alien element within the population. Against this, however, it should be noted that the grave goods, irrespective of their fineness, are always seen to be in the purely local traditions. Furthermore, two of these distinctive stone-lined graves were found in the cemetery of Tiwal esh-Sharqi, where they contained typical EB IV materials and were fully contemporary with the more numerous shaft tombs. The stone-built graves must be seen, therefore, as an indigenous feature, but perhaps representing the burial tradition of a very ancient, and otherwise entirely integrated strain within the population.

Contemporary textual sources which monitor Palestine's return to urban life during the Middle Bronze Age include the Egyptian execration texts, curses against various enemies, Asiatics, Nubians and Libyans, inscribed on clay vessels or statuettes and ritually smashed. They occur in two main groups, the first of which dates to the early Twelfth Dynasty, close to 2000 BC, and reflects an early stage in the process of re-urbanisation. Only a few towns are mentioned (Jerusalem, Ashkelon and Rehob in Palestine; Byblos, 'Arqat and Ullasa in Syria) but there are many names, otherwise unknown, which are thought to represent small communities or tribes. The second group of texts is later in date, late Twelfth Dynasty, and indicate that the urbanisation of Palestine was now well established for the texts refer to many well-known Middle Bronze Age sites.

The socio-political situation in the early part of the Middle Bronze Age is difficult to determine. That extensive trading with Egypt was re-established is clear from the

20. Early Bronze IV stone-lined grave at Tiwal esh-Sharqi, seen here after the initial surface clearance and with the large limestone covering slabs in position. (photo: PGD)

large number of imported Egyptian luxury goods found at sites throughout the country, but it is doubtful whether the Middle Kingdom pharaohs attempted to exercise any more enduring political control over the country.

Patriarchs and Hyksos

The foregoing discussion has tended to stress the essential continuity of the Palestinian population and its cultural attributes from the beginning of the Early Bronze Age through to the Middle Bronze Age. Now, if as most scholars would accept, the initial phase of the Middle Bronze Age (MB IIA) is to be seen as the formative stage in the development of the Canaanite civilisation of the second millennium, then on the basis of this continuity we must accept also that the Early Bronze Age, indeed as far back as the Proto-Urban, is equally 'Canaanite'. This is not to deny that small-scale population movements occurred throughout the whole of the third millennium BC. Internal demographic fluidity was undoubtedly responsible for bringing about a more or less uniform culture throughout the whole of the Levant in the Early Bronze, and perhaps even more so in the Middle Bronze Age. Small-scale and peaceful infiltrations from beyond the Levantine cultural continuum served only to enrich the culture and not in any way to destroy or replace it. It would be reasonable to suppose that these infiltrations might have increased during the Early Bronze IV period and during the very beginning of the Middle Bronze Age, when the whole of the Levant was in something of a state of flux, and the lack of any regional administrative control would have assisted free passage through whatever borders and polity zones had been established previously. It is against such a background that it might be thought reasonable to set into context the narratives relating to the biblical Patriarchs. The question of the historicity of the Patriarchal narratives is a complicated and largely unanswerable one. Archaeology cannot hope to prove the existence of Abraham or Isaac, nor indeed of any of the other characters referred to in the book of Genesis. On the other hand there is little reason to doubt in very general and very basic terms that the founding fathers of what was to become Israel might well have entered Palestine at some stage during the third or early second millennium. Unfortunately this is about all that can be said. For it must be appreciated that the stories relating to the Patriarchs were not put into their final form until some time between the seventh and fifth centuries BC. The source material drawn upon probably included historical texts, but it is unlikely that many, if any, of these were contemporary with the events described. In addition there were probably stories and folk legends transmitted through oral tradition, the content of which would have varied enormously in historical accuracy. A certain amount of fabrication and deliberate biasing of events should also be taken into account – material not unreasonably included in order to lift the spirits of the Israelite community in exile, and to reinforce the legitimacy of their claim to the land. Altogether, therefore, the accounts dealing with Abraham, Isaac, Joseph and Jacob, contain hundreds, perhaps even thousands, of individual strands only some of which are likely to bear any relation to the historical facts. In these circumstances it is hardly surprising that no consensus has been reached as to the time in which the events took place, let alone the historicity of the events themselves. The evidence of geographical and personal names referred to, and social institutions described, tends to be ambiguous. Scholars, finding close similarities between various of the social and tribal institutions described in Genesis, and those gleaned from the early second millennium texts found at the site of Mari on the Euphrates in Syria, have sought to place the 'Patriarchal period' in the early part of the Middle Bronze Age. Such a comparison is certainly valid, but since it is now possible to demonstrate cultural continuity from the beginning of the Early Bronze Age, there is nothing to suggest that these institutions had not existed in Palestine from the inception of that period.

Perhaps the most realistic approach to the Patriarchal stories is to assume that they contain elements of historical fact, but that these have been combined with less reliable material and assembled to create a coherent narrative concerning a fixed period of time, represented essentially by four generations. Isolating the individual elements leads to the conclusion that the events, in reality, took place over a very much longer period of time. References, for example, to the 'Cities of the Plain' represent, most probably, some of the most ancient traditions, for they presuppose the existence of an extensive occupation in the area at the southern end of the Dead Sea. Archaeological research

21. The development of the axehead: (*left*) a simple 'crescentic' axehead from the Amarneh cemetery dating to EB III (BM WA 116050); (*right*) the technologically accomplished EB IV development, the so-called 'fenestrated' axe (BM WA 136754); (*bottom right*) the MB IIA 'duckbill' variant of this type, from Sidon (BM WA 126978).

in this region, and principally the excavations at the sites of Bab edh-Dhrâ' and Numeira would require this extensive settlement phase to be placed in the first half of the third millennium BC, that is in EB II–III. Similar arguments can be adduced to suggest that perhaps the majority of the Patriarchal movements took place during the Early Bronze IV period, during which, as we have seen, conditions were most suited to the semi-sedentary pastoralist economy which seems to fit most clearly the descriptions of the biblical Patriarchs. At the other end of the scale, it would be tempting to set the stories of Joseph's experiences in Egypt against the background of the early part of the Middle Bronze Age. For here external documentation has provided evidence for the movement of Asiatics into the Egyptian Delta during this time. A wall-painting from the tomb of a nobleman at Beni Hasan, and dating to around 1900 BC, shows a party of Asiatics being introduced to the Egyptian court. Their Palestinian origin is clear from the weapons they carry, which include examples of the so-called 'duck-bill' axe, the distinctive Middle Bronze Age variant of the EB IV fenestrated axe mentioned above. More tangibly, excavations at various sites in the Egyptian Delta have revealed settlements and towns characterised by an almost purely Canaanite material culture, indicative indeed of a quite extensive influx of people from Palestine during the first quarter of the second millennium BC.

The incursions of Canaanites into the Egyptian Delta during the first phase of the Middle Bronze Age were undoubtedly responsible for the breakdown of centralised political control in Egypt and the collapse of the Middle Kingdom towards the end of the first quarter of the second millennium. In the chaos which followed, and which is known as the second intermediate period, it would appear that Asiatics, who must surely be identified as those Canaanites who had moved into Egypt early in the second millennium, seized political control in the Delta, establishing a local and independent dynasty. Known as the 'Hyksos' (from the Greek, meaning 'rulers of foreign lands') the kings of this Delta-based dynasty later came to exercise, for a brief period some form of control over the whole of Egypt, until they were eventually dispelled by a rival, native dynasty from Thebes. The Hyksos ruled from Avaris, a city identified with the archaeological site of Tell ed-Daba. Excavations here have revealed the prosperous nature of the capital city as well as the essentially Canaanite character of its material culture. In archaeological terms, the Hyksos rule in Egypt corresponds broadly with the second two phases of the Middle Bronze Age, MB IIB and C, dating approximately 1750–1550 BC.

Middle Bronze IIB–C: The Flowering of Canaanite Culture

What effect the Hyksos rule in Egypt had in Palestine is difficult to assess. It is unlikely that they had either the inclination or the ability to attempt any direct political control. Diplomatic relations, however, were presumably very close, and in these circumstances commercial ties would have been strengthened and expanded. This is surely reflected in the material culture of Palestine during the MB IIB–C period. For if MB IIA is seen (even if slightly erroneously – see above) as the formative period of Canaanite culture, then MB IIB–C bears witness to its full flowering. Indeed this period can be seen as the 'golden age' of Canaanite culture. Unhindered by the power struggles and foreign interventions that were to dominate the country's history in the second half of the millennium, Canaanite culture flourished unrestrained.

Architecture, art and craftsmanship achieved levels of accomplishment and sophistication which were to provide the ancient Near East with an enduring legacy well into the following millennium. The hoard of gold jewellery found at the site of Tell el-'Ajjul, for example, well illustrates the technological expertise and skill of the Canaanite craftsman, showing refined techniques of granulation and repoussée. Similar mastery is apparent in the unusually preserved wooden furniture from the Middle Bronze Age tombs at Jericho. Not only does the furniture display sophistication and elegance stylistically, but in terms of its construction it illustrates all of the advanced techniques of joinery employed by the modern carpenter. The MB IIB–C saw also the development of distinctive Canaanite

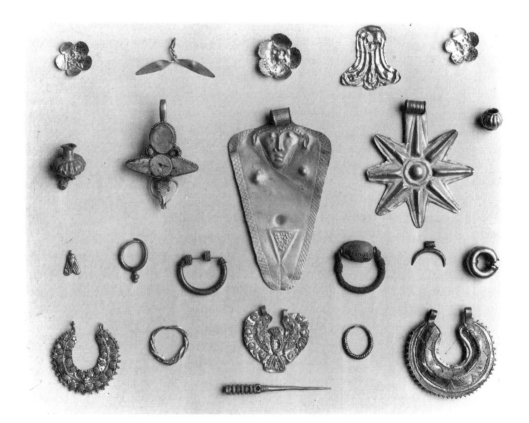

22. (*above*) Middle Bronze Age gold jewellery from Tell el-'Ajjul. (BM WA 130760–90)

23. (*top right*) Tomb H12 at Jericho, a large shaft tomb of the Middle Bronze Age, containing unusually preserved organic materials: vessels, baskets and wooden furniture. (photo: PGD)

24. (*bottom right*) Street and row of shops in Middle Bronze Age Jericho. (photo: PGD)

artistic traditions. The essence of Canaanite art is its eclecticism –
drawing elements from a whole variety of sources and countries,
and blending them together to form a totally coherent, aesthetically
satisfying whole. This is clearest perhaps in the realms of jewellery
and ivory carving, where individual motifs can be traced to Egypt,
Mesopotamia, Syria or the Aegean, and yet the resultant composition
is purely Canaanite. In this respect, of course, the Canaanites were
laying the foundations for the Phoenicians, their direct descendants,
whose artistic traditions were to so greatly enrich the Near Eastern
cultures of the first millennium BC.

The multi-faceted inspirational basis for the Canaanite art of the
Middle Bronze Age almost certainly developed as a response to
the ever increasing network of commercial relations. Trade with
Egypt must have been, as it had been in the Early Bronze Age, on
an extensive level. In addition, trading contacts were established
or strengthened with Syria and Anatolia and in particular
with Cyprus.

Intellectually, also, there is no reason to suppose that the
Canaanites were any less developed than their more opulent
(perhaps even ostentatious) neighbours. It was, after all, in Middle
Bronze Age Canaan that the first serious attempts were made
to devise a workable alphabetic writing system to replace the
outmoded and cumbersome syllabic cuneiform. Refined and only
slightly modified by the Phoenicians, it is essentially the same
alphabetic system that we use today.

The internal political structure of Palestine during the
Middle Bronze Age is largely unknown. On analogy with the
Early Bronze Age, however, it would seem likely that the
country was composed of a large number of independent city
states, each ruled by a dynast or prince. Each large urban
centre, the nucleus of the state, would have controlled an area
of land containing a number of dependent towns and villages.
It is possible that from time to time groups of city states formed
loose confederations, and there is some evidence to suggest that
during the latter part of the Middle Bronze Age, the large and
powerful city of Hazor exercised some degree of hegemony over
the cities in the north of the country. Interstate quarrels and conflicts
must not have been uncommon. The expanding economy with
fiercely competitive markets brought a new prosperity to Middle

25. (*right*) Middle Bronze Age dagger from Lachish bearing four incised early alphabetic
signs (Israel Museum/photo: BM/WT)

Bronze Age Palestine, but as a consequence this undoubtedly led to bitter rivalries between cities. Furthermore, the accumulation of wealth required protection, and it is hardly surprising, therefore, that this period saw the development of a distinctive type of fortification system which appears to have been applied in more or less the same form to nearly every major site in Palestine. Known variously as the 'rampart' or 'glacis' or 'Hyksos glacis' fortification system, it was, in reality, only partly defensive in function. For it has to be appreciated that by the time of the Middle Bronze Age many of the major sites, which had been occupied nearly continuously since the Proto-Urban period (and sometimes before), with successive settlements utilising for the most part mud-brick as a construction material, had risen as great mounds of accumulated debris to considerable heights. As such, these mounds (or *tells*) were becoming unstable and required some form of consolidation especially around the sides. This is precisely what was done during the Middle Bronze IIB period (or perhaps slightly before). The sides of the city mound were regularised and consolidated, and in order to enhance the already defensive aspect of the steep slopes, a coating of plaster was applied to achieve the so-called 'glacis'. At the top of the glacis, a tall earthen rampart was constructed which was then crowned with the city wall itself. The base of the glacis was retained by a strong revetment wall, and the defensive measures were completed by the digging of a deep encircling ditch or 'fosse' around the base of the mound. It should be noted that this type of defensive system, often cited as one of the most characteristic features of Middle Bronze Palestine, can again trace its origins back to the Early Bronze Age.

Egyptian Domination: The Late Bronze Age

During the sixteenth century BC, Theban opposition to the Hyksos rule grew ever stronger, and the pharaohs of the native Seventeenth Dynasty actively campaigned to expel them. Kamose managed to restrict their sphere of influence to the eastern Delta, following a campaign in about 1577 BC which brought him close to the city of Avaris itself. It was his brother Ahmose (1570–1546 BC), however, who finally managed to drive the Hyksos out of Egypt some ten years later. Expelled from Egypt, the Hyksos sought refuge in the strongly fortified cities of Canaan. The pharaohs of the Eighteenth Dynasty were not about to leave the issue there. Partly for punitive reasons, but more probably mainly in order to ensure that no other Asiatic invader could attempt to usurp power in Egypt, the Egyptian army embarked on a series of almost annual campaigns in Palestine. The city of Sharuhen (identified as Tell Fara) was laid siege to for nearly three years before finally succumbing to the Egyptian forces. Following its capture, little seems to have stood in the way of the Egyptian advance.

The archaeological record bears witness to the devastating effect of these vigorous campaigns. The end of the Middle Bronze Age (c.1550) is marked by a series of destructions as city after city fell to the Egyptian armies. Tuthmosis I (1525–c.1512 BC) swept through Palestine and on into Syria, reaching even the Euphrates, where he erected a stele. Control of Syria could not, however, be sustained. Strong opposition to the Egyptian advance came from the Hurrian city states of that country, then under the control of Mitanni. A coalition of Syrian and Canaanite states met the armies of Tuthmosis III (1504–1450 BC) at Megiddo in 1470. The battle ended in a decisive victory for the Egyptians and one which, after a brilliant series of follow-up campaigns, gave them undisputed control of Palestine and much of coastal and south-central Syria. Thus, Egypt's Asiatic empire was created. The city states of Palestine were subjected to firm Egyptian control with their native princes treated as vassals of the pharaoh. The taxation imposed by the Egyptian administration must have been burdensome, but in return, the Canaanite cities gained security and protection. Canaanite culture in the Late Bronze Age continued to flourish as it had done in the previous period, now enriched by the even greater commercial and cultural contacts provided by the Egyptians. Large numbers of Egyptian luxury items entered the country – ivories, glazed vessels, objects of faience, and presumably carved wood objects that have not been preserved. The benefits were not all in one direction, and Canaanite products entering Egypt exerted a marked influence on the material culture of the New Kingdom. Canaanite artistry and craftsmanship were highly prized and it is slightly ironical that objects which had themselves been inspired by Egyptian prototypes, were manufactured in Canaan for export to Egypt. Trading centres with Cyprus and the Aegean were further developed. Large numbers of imported Cypriote pottery vessels have been found in excavations throughout Palestine, and towards

26. (*left*) Late Bronze Age 'bichrome ware' krater from Lachish. (BM WA 160152)

27. (*right*) Two Late Bronze Age necklaces from Lachish, both showing strong Egyptian influence. (BM WA 132125–6)

the end of the period in question, these are supplemented by fine Mycenaean wares. Some of these vessels may have been imported in their own right as luxury items or table wares, but many were clearly imported with contents intact. Residual analysis has shown, for example, that some of the Mycenaean vessels (stirrup jars and pyxides) were used to transport perfumed oils and in the case of a little Cypriote juglet type, bearing a striking resemblance to an inverted poppy head, the contents have been analysed as opium.

Egypt's grip on the empire weakened somewhat during the fourteenth century BC. Akhenaten (1379–1362 BC), perhaps more preoccupied with religious reforms than with the government of the empire, failed to take account of the changing political situation in the north, where the energetic and aggressive Hittite empire had moved into the

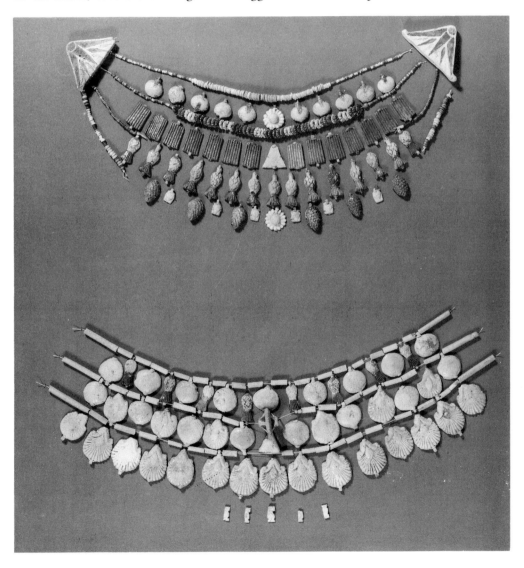

power vacuum left by the decline of Mitanni. The territorial gains in Syria made by Tuthmosis III at the battle of Megiddo were lost to the Hittites, and in Palestine the visible weakness of the Egyptian administration was perceived as an opportunity for local rulers to rebel or become engaged in quarrels and feuds with their neighbours. This period of conflict and instability is wonderfully illustrated by the so-called Amarna letters, clay tablets written in Babylonian cuneiform which were found in the archives of Akhenaten's capital at Tell el-Amarna. They represent the diplomatic correspondence sent by various vassal princes of the empire to the Egyptian pharaohs Amenophis III, Akhenaten (Amenophis IV) and Tutankhamun. In the letters the rulers proclaim their loyalty to pharaoh, discuss international affairs and local problems (often followed by requests for military aid) and most vigorously accuse their neighbours of disloyalty.

It is in the Amarna correspondence that we also encounter references to lawless groups of bandits, criminals and social misfits who are termed *Hapiru*. Sometimes it seems they were engaged as mercenaries employed by the ruler of one city state in order to menace and terrorise another. More often, however, they are represented as roaming bands, bound in independent communal or semi-tribal organisations, and living on the fringes of civilised society, to which they posed a constant threat. It would be tempting, perhaps, to equate these *Hapiru* with the biblical Hebrews, but additional textual sources

28. (*top left*) Late Bronze Age imported Cypriote vessels from Gezer, including a bull rhyton. (BM WA collections)

29. (*bottom left*) Late Bronze Age imported Mycenaean vessels and local imitations from Gezer. (BM WA collections)

30. (*right*) Amarna Letter No. 68. This clay tablet inscribed in cuneiform is from Shuwardata, the ruler of Hebron, and in it he tells the pharoah that he stands alone and needs a large force to rescue him. (BM WA E29851)

(Babylonian, Ugaritic and Hittite) which also refer to the *Hapiru,* not only demonstrate that their sphere of activity was not confined solely to Canaan, but more significantly, make it clear that they had no single identity. In other words, *Hapiru* cannot be seen as an ethnolinguistic term, specifying a particular people, but rather it should be seen as a more general term for dispossessed or homeless people of varying ethnic backgrounds. In these terms people could become *Hapiru* by virtue of unfortunate circumstances. In all probability, therefore, there was a direct connection between the *Hapiru* and the Hebrews in as far as the Hebrews were undoubtedly *Hapiru:* not all *Hapiru,* on the other hand, were Hebrews.

The Egyptian Eighteenth Dynasty ended with Horemheb (1348–1320 BC), an army general who, lacking an heir, appointed his vizier, Ramesses to succeed him. Ramesses I became, therefore founder of the Nineteenth Dynasty and he, together with his co-regent Seti I (1318–1304 BC) set about re-establishing firm control throughout the Asiatic empire. In addition to bringing to heel rebellious rulers in Canaan, the main thrust of their foreign policy was directed towards containing Hittite expansion in Syria. Seti I, in fact, managed to conclude a treaty with the Hittites, but this proved to be short lived, and it was left to his son, Ramesses II (1304–1237 BC) to bring about a lasting peace settlement following the hard-fought battle of Qadesh in 1289 BC. The treaty that was eventually signed, not, it may be added, until some sixteen years after the battle of Qadesh, led to a period of peace and prosperity in Egypt that was marked by extensive and elaborate building programmes. A new capital was built in the eastern Delta, Per-Ramesses, which, together with the city of Pithom (Per-Atum, tentatively identified as Tell el-Maskhuta) is said in the book of Exodus to have been built using Hebrew labour. It is important to note that despite the reservation regarding the *Hapiru*/Hebrew equation given above, the Egyptian Papyrus Leiden 348 records that *Hapiru,* together with soldiers, were employed in dragging stones for the construction of the gateway pylons of one of Ramesses II monumental buildings, the *Hapiru* having been presumably rounded up and taken prisoner during the Amarna period or during the campaigns of Seti I. Certainly this apparent coincidence of Hebrews and *Hapiru* in large-scale building programmes of Ramesses II cannot be dismissed, and it may well be that the Hebrews of the exodus were indeed drawn from the *Hapiru.* Furthermore, it would seem reasonable to conclude under these circumstances, that Ramesses II was the unnamed pharaoh of the exodus and oppressor of the Israelite people.

It was probably also Ramesses II who was responsible for a major reorganisation of the Egyptian empire in Canaan. For he seems to have instituted a deliberate policy of winding down certain cities which were considered to be superfluous to the needs of the empire, and, at the same time, strengthening or refounding others which were seen as strategically vital. This process continued and perhaps even increased during the early part of the Twentieth Dynasty. The results of this policy, as seen in the archaeological record used to be taken as evidence for a dramatic cultural decline at the end of the Late Bronze Age. The reality of the situation actually demonstrates the reverse. For although it is certainly true that certain sites such as Bethel and Hazor were abandoned, others were revitalised and took on an even more strongly Egyptian aspect than before. Sites such as Gaza in the south of the country and Beth Shan in the north became major centres of what may be seen as an Egyptian chain of command. Sites were selected for strategic reasons, both militarily and probably also in an economic sense, and it is clear that in both respects Egypt was anxious to safeguard her interests. Tightly defended by a chain of forts and way-stations were the so-called 'Ways of Horus', the main route linking Egypt with southern Canaan by way of Sinai. Excavations at Deir el-Balah, which was the last way-station on the road before Gaza, have revealed the strongly Egyptian character of the architecture. A new type of building appeared at the major centres of Egyptian control throughout Canaan. Termed the 'Egyptian Governor's Residency',

31. Statue of Ramesses II,
most probably the pharoah of
the biblical exodus. (BM EA 96)

it was a large square-plan public building divided into storerooms and courtyards. More significant than the plan, however, is the fact that the construction method is purely Egyptian with massively deep brick foundations rather than the usual stone, and exterior walls often built as pairs with a channel between them. These residencies have been identified at sites such as Tell el-Far'ah, Tell Sera, Beth Shan and Aphek. Most interesting of all, perhaps, was the discovery of such a residency building at Tell es-Sa'idiyeh, east of the river Jordan, a site which seems to have been refounded during the reign of Ramesses II.

The key sites in the re-organised empire not only served as administrative centres, but also controlled military resources. Permanent garrisons of Egyptian troops were maintained at Gaza and Beth Shan, and probably at a number of other bases as well. In addition to Egyptian forces there were undoubtedly foreign contingents, people of Aegean or southern Anatolian origin known as the Sea Peoples, the best-known group of which are the Philistines. Although the Philistines themselves are not recorded in the Egyptian sources until the time of their invasion during the reign of Ramesses III, other groups of Sea Peoples, most prominently Sherden, are encountered in the fourteenth century Amarna Letters. Depicted as raiders or pirates, these people were defeated in battle early in the reign of Ramesses II, and were subsequently pressed into service in the Egyptian Army. Sherden troops fought alongside the Egyptians at the battle of Qadesh. The peculiar clay anthropoid coffins found at Beth Shan, Deir el-Balah, and Lachish should probably

32. (*left*) Face cover from an anthropoid clay coffin from Tomb 570 at Lachish. Such coffins might well have been used by Sea Peoples personnel serving with the Egyptians. (BM WA 160212)

33. (*right*) The so-called 'Fosse Temple' at Lachish, a small Late Bronze Age Canaanite sanctuary built in the disused Middle Bronze Age defensive ditch (or fosse). This building and its contents have provided a wealth of information relating to Canaanite cult practices. (photo: BM/WT)

be identified as burial containers for such Sea Peoples' forces, and a similar interpretation would seem appropriate for the distinctive and functionally related double pithos burials found in the cemetery at Tell es-Sa'idiyeh.

The changed aspect of the Egyptian empire at the end of the Late Bronze Age had a profound and far-reaching effect within Canaan itself. For the selectivity of the re-organisation, in which only certain sites were allowed to prosper, meant effectively the demise of others. There must have been, therefore, a very great increase in the numbers of dispossessed or homeless peoples. It is likely that many of these people moved to the hill country, where a sharp increase in small village settlements can be observed at this time. The demographic dimorphism that ensued was to prove instrumental in the formation of early Israel. Indeed, the reference to 'Israel' as a socio-political entity on the victory stele of the pharaoh Merneptah (1235–1223 BC) should be interpreted as a recognition of this population split – the urban Egypto-Canaanite polities on the one hand, and a coalition of dispossessed Canaanites now occupying the hill country, on the other: in the eyes of the Egyptians the latter would certainly have been seen as *Hapiru*.

Before pursuing the rise of the Israelite kingdom, however, a third important element has to be introduced into the general confusion that engulfs the end of the second millennium BC. In the fifth year of pharaoh Merneptah groups of Sea Peoples allied themselves with the Libyans in an attack on Egypt. In addition to the ubiquitous Sherden, other

groups named are the Shekelesh, Lukka, Teresh and Ekwesh. The attack was repulsed and the victory was celebrated in poetic form on a stele which also recounts Merneptah's campaign against the cities of Ashkelon and Gezer and, as mentioned above, 'Israel'. The Sea Peoples' threat was not, however, eliminated and it is likely that they continued to menace the Egyptian borders throughout the remaining years of Merneptah's reign and through the uneasy period which marked the transition from the Nineteenth to the Twentieth Dynasties following his death in 1223 BC.

The situation came to a head in the reign of Ramesses III (1198–1166 BC), the last great pharaoh of the New Kingdom. In the eighth year of his reign, two great battles were fought against leagues of Sea Peoples, the accounts of which are described and vividly illustrated on the reliefs from the walls of Ramesses' mortuary temple at Medinet Habu. One of the battles was fought on land and took place in *Djahi* (the Egyptian name for the Phoenician coast and hinterland down to Palestine). According to the text of the reliefs the leagues of the Sea Peoples comprised Philistines, Shekelesh, Denyen, Tjeker and Weshesh. They are shown as fighting in chariots, with their families accompanying them in ox-drawn carts with solid wheels. It is interesting to observe that the Sherden, themselves of course Sea Peoples, took part in the battle on the Egyptian side. They can be identified on the reliefs by means of their distinctive horned helmets. Ramesses claimed a decisive victory and took many captives. Some of these were undoubtedly pressed into military service and were used to man the garrisons at the Egyptian control centres in Canaan, cities such as Beth Shan, Tell el-Far'ah, Lachish and Gezer. The later group of anthropoid clay coffins found in the northern cemetery at Beth Shan can very plausibly be related to these foreign troops. Indeed, many of the coffins bear representations of the type of feathered headdress which occurs on the Medinet Habu reliefs and which can be identified as belonging to the Philistines, Tjeker and Denyen.

For all Ramesses' claim, however, the battle cannot have been as decisive as all that. For the Sea Peoples were soon able to launch a major naval attack on the Egyptian Delta, apparently within the same year (year 8). The reliefs dealing with this battle show the Sea Peoples in their fighting ships, vessels with duck-shaped prow and stern, and powered apparently only by sail. The Sherden in this case are seen to be fighting with the other Sea Peoples against the Egyptians, but from our previous knowledge, it would seem likely that in reality, the Sherden were fighting on both sides. Again, Ramesses claimed a victory over the Sea Peoples, and this was probably the case in as far as they were repulsed from the shores of Egypt itself. The defeated Sea Peoples were, in the event, thrown back on to the coast of Palestine, where they settled. It is unlikely that Egypt had any choice in this matter, for the Asiatic empire was beginning to crumble, and the effects of the wars must have had a crippling effect on the economy.

The arrival of the Philistines and other Sea Peoples on the coast of Palestine at the beginning of the twelfth century has traditionally been taken as the transition from the Late Bronze to the Iron Age. In one respect this is reasonable, in that the Sea Peoples certainly did develop the iron industry on a large scale. The majority of iron artifacts found in twelfth-century contexts are from sites controlled by, or heavily influenced by, the Sea Peoples. In other respects, however, the creation of a break at 1200 BC is unfortunate and misleading, for it bears no relation to the socio-political situation in the country. For, as we have seen, although many sites in Canaan were abandoned before 1200 BC as a part of the deliberate process of rationalisation of the empire in the Nineteenth and Twentieth Dynasties, other key sites continued to flourish and expand, and to exhibit the same Egypto-Canaanite culture as in the earlier phases of the Late Bronze Age. These sites were not destroyed, abandoned, nor in any way eclipsed until the final withdrawal of Egyptian control, which can be set around the middle of the twelfth century BC, during the reigns of Ramesses V or VI. It was the withdrawal of Egypt's presence from Canaan in the mid-twelfth century which provided the opportunity for both the Philistine expansion and the growth of the Israelite nation. In most respects, therefore, 1150 BC is much to be preferred as a date at which to set the transition from the Late Bronze Age to the Iron Age.

The Iron Age and the Rise of Israel

By about 1150 BC the political and demographic configuration of Palestine had changed completely. Egypt had effectively left the scene, and the vacuum created by its absence was ready to be filled by the inheritors of its empire, the Sea Peoples, most prominently the Philistines on the one hand, and the Israelites on the other.

The rise of Israel as a political entity has been hinted at in the previous section. Its origins undoubtedly lay in the restructuring of the Egyptian empire by the pharaohs of the Nineteenth Dynasty. This process which led to the demise of many strategically insignificant cities and towns, released large numbers of dispossessed and homeless Canaanites. Many of them moved to the hill country where they established small farming villages. Others undoubtedly opted for a semi-sedentary life, pursuing pastoralism as a means of gaining a living. In any event, by the very act of becoming non-urbanised these Canaanites had effectively become, in the eyes of the Egyptians, *Hapiru*. By the time of Merneptah, the population in the hill country had grown to such an extent that it was recognised as a socio-political entity, and was referred to as 'Israel'. The core of the later Israelite nation lay, therefore, in the farming communities of the hill country of Palestine, which were until the mid-twelfth century BC contemporary with, yet almost mutually exclusive from, the powerful Egyptian controlled city states of Canaan.

The historicity of the biblical narratives relating to the exodus is still much debated, and no real consensus has yet emerged. The problems concerning the diversity, nature and reliability of the source material used in the compilation of the stories are much the same, and every bit as complex as those relating to the biblical Patriarchs (see above). The results of archaeological research have, in a sense compounded the problems, for they have demonstrated, as we have seen, that the story of the exodus is no longer required in order to explain the birth and growth of the Israelite nation. This statement should not be seen however, as a justification for rejecting the Exodus narratives out of hand. Indeed there is good reason to accept that the core of the exodus story is rooted in reality. Egyptian textual sources have provided clear evidence that *Hapiru* were taken as prisoners during the campaigns of Seti I and possibly earlier. They have further shown that *Hapiru* were employed in large-scale public-building projects in Egypt during the reign of Ramesses II. Given these circumstances, there is every reason to believe that a group of such *Hapiru* might well have been led out of Egypt by a forceful and charismatic figure and brought eventually to Palestine. Once in the country they would surely have joined the village communities in the hill country. This view may appear minimalist, but in terms of the archaeological evidence, it is all that can be safely proposed.

A similar standpoint must also be adopted with regard to the conquest of the land by Joshua. The archaeological evidence presented in the foregoing discussion makes it quite clear that a military conquest on a wide scale under whatever leader, would have been simply out of the question prior to the withdrawal of Egyptian control in the mid-twelfth century BC. Indeed, this is not denied in the biblical accounts: both the books of Joshua and Judges, having discussed the capture of several towns, most of which lay in the hill country, list a large number of unconquered Canaanite cities. Instead, therefore, Joshua's conquest must be seen in the context of the very restricted area to which the stories relate, and in which most of the cities said to have been conquered were not, in fact, occupied at the time. Joshua's conquest in this region was no less real, however, but it was surely largely ideological, involving the 'winning over' of the hill country's communities to radically new and different religious concepts.

It was only after the collapse of the Egyptian empire in the middle of the twelfth century BC that Israel was able to expand beyond the borders of the hill country. Again, however, to what extent this was a deliberate aggressive policy involving military exploits, and to what extent it came about as a natural process of integration with those Canaanite cities now freed from their Egyptian overlords, is difficult to access. On the one hand, these once powerful cities now severely weakened by the withdrawal of their defensive garrisons, and economically impoverished from the cessation of Egyptian provisioning, would have been far more susceptible to attack. On the other hand, despite the many years of service to the Egyptians, the Canaanite population that remained, in reality consisted of the same people as those who had sought refuge in the hill country a century or so before, and it is possible that some degree of kinship was recognised.

To a large extent this question is academic, since any expansionist aims the Israelites might have had were curbed, and held in check by those of the Philistines. Since the time of their settlement on the coast of Palestine, following the land and sea battles in Ramesses III's reign, the Sea Peoples, including the Philistines, had consolidated their position. The Onomasticon of Amenope, which dates to the end of the twelfth or beginning of the eleventh century records the areas settled by the Sea Peoples in Palestine within the sphere of Egyptian influence. The document refers to various cities, and three ethnic groups, the Sherden, the Tjeker and the Philistines. Unfortunately, only in the case of the last named group, the Philistines, are specific cities attributed to their control, the cities of Gaza, Ashkelon and Ashdod. The concentration of Philistines on the southern Palestinian coast is confirmed by both the biblical accounts and by the 'Tale of Wen Amun', a mid-eleventh century Egyptian account of an expedition to Byblos to purchase timber. This story is invaluable, for not only does it locate the area of the Tjeker settlement as being to the north of Philistia, centred on the city of Dor, but also, and more importantly, it clearly illustrates Egypt's inability to exercise any real control whatever over this area which had formerly been the mainstay of her empire. Although, according to Wen Amun, the Tjeker king, Beder, acknowledged the Egyptian rule, this was in reality a political fiction, and the same was undoubtedly true of the Philistines as well. Of the settlement of the other Sea Peoples, the Sherden and those adversaries of Egypt referred to in the Onomasticon of Amenope, little can be said. There is certain support from the biblical sources, however, for the notion that the

34. Philistine jug from Tell Fara. (BM WA L69; on loan from the Petrie collection)

Denyen might have settled in the region of ancient Laish (Tell Dan) and subsequently were absorbed into Israelite historical tradition as the 'tribe of Dan'. The book of Judges, for example refers to Dan in relation to its ships (Judges 5:17), surely something of an anomaly in the context of the Israelite tribes?

The later history of the Sea Peoples in Palestine becomes effectively the history of the Philistines, for little is known of the others, and there is no means of knowing to what extent they maintained individual identities. An independent status for the Tjeker would seem to be assured until the mid-eleventh century BC by the Wen Amun Tale, but the Bible on the other hand, speaks only of the Philistines.

The arrival of the Philistines on the coast of Palestine at the start of the twelfth century BC can be witnessed in the archaeological record, not only by a series of destructions at formerly Canaanite sites, but also by the subsequent development of a distinctive material culture. Initially, immediately following their settlement, the Philistines produced a local variety of a contemporary style of Mycenaean pottery. This, in the context of the prevailing Egypto-Canaanite wares of the Late Bronze Age tradition, and the excessively drab Israelite early Iron Age pottery, might be considered distinctive enough, but it was nothing compared with the development which took place some fifty years later, when the 'Philistine style' emerged. This wonderful pottery, artistically inspired, combined in a unique painted style, motifs derived from Egyptian, Canaanite and Mycenaean traditions. There are very few cases in which archaeologists are able to tie pots to people with any degree of certainty. In the case of the Philistine pottery, however, the relationship is secure, and indeed this has provided the means by which it has been possible to chart the progress and expansion of the Philistines subsequent to their initial settlement. Not only did the Philistines introduce a new and characteristic style of pottery to Palestine. New styles of architecture have also be found, and the temples in particular strongly reflect the Aegean background and origin of the Philistines themselves. This same background is apparent, too, in many of the other artifacts associated with the Philistines: cult objects, terracottas and metalwork.

For nearly a hundred years the Philistines and the Israelites lived side by side, the Philistines in the rich coastal plain, the Israelites in the more barren hill country. During the eleventh century, however, the Philistines embarked on a programme of expansion, and attempted to exert control over the hill country. Thus began a period of oppression, the events of which are vividly described in the Bible. This period, which lasted from about 1080–1030 BC, was of crucial importance for Israel, for the Philistine threat provided the impetus necessary to weld together the fragmented and semi-independent communities of Israelites into a single nation. This process was begun by Saul, who can be seen as the first charismatic leader of Israel, and if his accomplishments are portrayed as having been somewhat variable, at the very least, he laid the groundwork for the more impressive achievements of his successor David.

Having, in this brief survey, brought Palestine from the Neolithic of the eighth millennium BC through the complexities of the Early, Middle and Late Bronze Ages and into the Iron Age of the first millennium, and delivered it, so to speak, into the hands of

Saul, the remaining history of the Israelite nation can be described more briefly. For the period from the founding of the nation right through to the exile and restoration is thoroughly and brilliantly documented by the historical books of the Old Testament. Furthermore, in many instances, these events can be corroborated by external sources, principally Egyptian, Assyrian and Babylonian, and frequently also by contemporary internal ones: inscriptions in ancient Hebrew, Moabite, Phoenician, and Aramaic.

With regard to the material culture of the Iron Age, the Canaanite ancestry of the Israelites is evident in nearly all of its aspects. The traditions established in the Middle and Late Bronze Ages continued to develop smoothly and logically throughout the entire span of the Iron Age, and well into the Hellenistic era. Pottery, metalwork, and domestic, public, religious and military architecture, all display essential continuity. What the Israelites clearly lacked, however, was artistic excellence, or indeed inspiration, and their material culture is, therefore, seen to be extraordinarily drab by comparison with what had preceded it. This deficiency had most probably resulted primarily from the necessarily mundane lifestyle of the Israelites in the hill country, and secondarily, from the Egyptians having, in all likelihood, taken the cream of Canaanite artists and craftsmen with them when they withdrew from the country in the mid-twelfth century. Only in Phoenicia, which was, in effect, a Canaanite enclave on the Syrian coast, were the aesthetic ideals of the second millennium BC upheld and indeed built upon throughout the first. Not infrequently did the Israelites themselves call upon the craft and artistic expertise of the Phoenicians whenever significant monuments or buildings were designed.

If the cultural history of Palestine in the Iron Age appears from the foregoing statement to be somewhat dull, the political history is far from being so. In many respects it was David rather than Saul who should be seen as the founder of the Israelite nation, for it was he, in about 1000 BC, who captured the Jebusite city of Jerusalem, and united in a personal monarchy the separate groups of Israelite clans and confederations. Through a combination of military skill and intelligent diplomacy, David extended the borders of Israel to include the southern part of Syria (territory formerly held by the Aramaean kingdom of Damascus), the kingdoms of Ammon and Moab in Transjordan, and part of the northern Negev. In addition, he established an important alliance with Phoenicia. Solomon, in the second half of the tenth century BC, attempted to consolidate these gains through military building and by the establishment of an effective civil organisation, but even during his lifetime, much of the territory taken by David was lost. The kingdom, nevertheless flourished, due in large part to the establishment of imaginative and wide-spread trading relations with Phoenicia, Egypt, Africa and Arabia. Perhaps Solomon's greatest accomplishment, however, was the establishment of Jerusalem as the kingdom's capital, and the construction there of the great Temple.

An uneasy tension between north and south had existed in the country since the reign of Saul, and following Solomon's death in 928 BC, his son Rehoboam's refusal to acknowledge various grievances of the north led to the development of a major rift between the two areas, and the subsequent division of the monarchy, Judah in the south and Israel in the north. Jeroboam, a northerner who had been banished by Solomon

35. Ivory furniture inlays from Ahab's palace at Samaria. (BM WA L31–48; on loan from the Palestine Exploration Fund)

for dissident activities, and had taken refuge in Egypt during his reign, was proclaimed king of Israel. To make matters worse, in 924 BC, on the pretext of supporting Jeroboam's claim, the Egyptian pharaoh Sheshonq I, founder of the Twenty-second Dynasty, launched a major campaign in Palestine. The biblical account of this bitter and punitive raid in the Book of Kings refers to the capture of cities in Judah and the receiving of the Temple and palace treasures from Jerusalem. This can be complimented, however by Sheshonq's own account, preserved on the walls of the great temple of Amun at Karnak, which makes it quite clear that the attack was directed not only at Judah but also at Israel.

The capital of the southern kingdom remained at Jerusalem throughout its history. The northern kingdom of Israel initially made Tirzah (Tell el-Far'ah) its capital, but under Omri, some sixty years later, the capital was moved to Samaria.

The two kingdoms of Israel and Judah lived side by side in a rather uneasy relationship for nearly 200 years, sometimes at war with one another, sometimes in alliance. The major threat to both kingdoms came, however, from the rising power of Assyria, intent on extending its empire westwards towards the Mediterranean. During the ninth century, Assyria's ambitions were temporarily held in check by an impressive coalition of Levantine states at the battle of Qarqar in 853. This consisted of the kings of Damascus and Hamath, together with the king Ahab of Israel, and further support came from troops of various Phoenician city states, an Egyptian force, and a contingent of Arabs mounted on camels. Although the Assyrian king Shalmaneser III claimed a victory at Qarqar, the resistance of the coalition must have been such that Shalmaneser was unable to press forward. The respite, however, was brief: Shalmaneser returned in 641, reaching first Damascus, and from there marched south through the Hauran and into Israelite territory. Submission was exacted from the Israelite king, Jehu, who is depicted on the Black Obelisk paying tribute to the Assyrian king.

During the first half of the eighth century, Assyria, perhaps preoccupied with the increasing threat of Urartu to the north, relaxed its pressure on Israel, providing a welcome period of prosperity, during which Jeroboam II (786–746) was even able to capture Damascus. The situation changed, however, under Tiglath Pileser III (744–727), a vigorous and innovative ruler who, instead of seeing the conquered regions merely as tribute-paying vassals, turned them into directly ruled administrative provinces. During his reign, a chain of such provinces was established

36. Limestone stele of Shalmaneser III from Kurkh (south-eastern Turkey). The text includes a description of Shalmaneser's defeat of a coalition of Asiatic rulers at Qarqar on the Orontes in 853 BC. The coalition included King Ahab of Israel. (BM WA 118884)

as far south as Damascus, with Israel partly under provincial administration and partly tributary. His successors, Shalmaneser V (726–722) and Sargon II (721–705) extended Assyrian control in Syria and Palestine. The northern kingdom of Israel came to an end as an independent state in 722 with the capture of Samaria and loss of part of its population through the Assyrian policy of deportation. The southern kingdom of Judah was forced into a totally submissive position, and although Hezekiah (715–687/6) rebelled against the Assyrian king Sennacherib in 701 BC, the attempt was a disaster. Jerusalem itself was not taken, but the great city of Lachish was laid siege to and fell to the Assyrian king. The details of the siege and attack on Lachish are vividly illustrated on the series of limestone reliefs from Sennacherib's palace at Nineveh, which are now on permanent display in the British Museum.

With Sennacherib and his son and successor, Esarhaddon (680–669), Assyria had reached its peak; subsequent rulers were less able, and by 625 BC Babylon had thrown off the Assyrian yoke. Judah made a bid for independence and under Josiah (641–609 BC) extended

37. (*top left*) Detail from the Black Obelisk of Shalmaneser III, showing the Israelite tribute (the kneeling figure may not necessarily be Jehu himself). (BM WA 118885)

38. (*bottom left*) Part of the Siege of Lachish reliefs from Sennacherib's palace at Nineveh, showing the Assyrian attack on the city in 701 BC. (BM WA 124902–15)

39. (*below*) Reconstruction drawing of Lachish as it might have appeared at the time of the Assyrian attack in 701 BC. The drawing by H. H. McWilliams was based on aerial photographs and field plans of the excavated remains. (photo: BM/WT)

its territory northwards and westwards, perhaps in an attempt to emulate the former glories of David and Solomon's reigns. This was to be the 'Swan Song' of Judah. The Assyrian capital Nineveh fell to the Babylonians in 612 BC, and Josiah died in a clash with the Egyptians, who in 609 embarked on a campaign to stem the tide of the Babylonian advance. For a few years Judah came under Egyptian control, but in 605 the Babylonian king Nebuchadnezzar defeated the Egyptians at Carchemish, and four years later, a further battle in the Gaza plain not only finally removed the Egyptian threat from Asia, but also placed Judah firmly in Babylonian control.

Jehoiakim (609–598) soon rebelled, however, pledging allegiance to Egypt, an act which gave the Babylonians an excuse to invade the country. In 598 BC Nebuchadnezzar raided Judah, captured Jerusalem and deported the royal family, installing on the throne a 'puppet', Zedekiah, the former king's uncle. Zedekiah was, however, a weak ruler, quite unable to control the internal unrest and sedition, and rebellion broke out again. Nebuchadnezzar was quick to act, and showed no mercy. In the campaign of 587, which was to bring about the destruction of Jerusalem and the end of the southern kingdom of Judah, Lachish and nearby Azekah (Tell Zakariyah) were the last two cities to be subdued. The archaeological evidence fully supports the historical record, for everywhere in the excavated areas were found the signs of extensive burning. The last few days before the fall of Lachish are poignantly documented by a group of ostraca, letters written on potsherds in black ink, discovered among the burnt debris of the guardroom between the inner and outer city gate. They are written in ancient Hebrew script, and are mostly addressed to the military commander of Lachish, Ya'ush. They were sent from an officer named Hosha'yahu, who was in charge of a military outpost positioned somewhere

40. (*left*) Lachish Letter II, which may be read: 'May Yahweh cause my lord to hear news of peace, even now, even now. Who is your servant but a dog that my lord should remember his servant?' (translation by T. C. Mitchell). (BM WA 125702)

41. (*top right*) Group of thirty children sieving the excavated soil following the initial discovery of the Lachish Letters in 1934. (photo: BM/WT)

42. (*bottom right*) Clay cylinder inscribed in Babylonian cuneiform containing a text of Cyrus the Great, King of Persia from 549 to 530 BC. (BM WA 90920)

between Lachish and Azekah. Most ominous of all is letter IV (now in the Rockefeller Museum, Jerusalem) which contains the lines 'we are waiting for the signal-fires of Lachish, according to all the signs which my lord gives, for we no longer see the signals of Azekah': the implications are clear.

The total subjugation of Judah which followed Nebuchadnezzar's campaign of 587 BC was accompanied by the large-scale deportation of part of its population. Thus began the exile, a period of great significance for the Jews spiritually, and one which would profoundly influence later religious ideology and teaching.

It was during the reign of Cyrus, the Persian ruler who had inherited the Babylonian empire following the defeat of Nabonidus and his co-regent Belshazzar in 539 BC, that the Jews were allowed to return to Israel. The rebuilding of the city of Jerusalem and its Temple are fully described in the books of Ezra and Nehemiah. In other respects, relatively little is known of Palestine during the Persian period (c.539–332 BC). It was included within the satrapy called 'Beyond the River' and within this large administrative unit, Judah appears to have been organised into at least five districts.

Archaeologically, the Persian period is only beginning to emerge from a period of relative obscurity, thanks to a number of more recent excavations. The material culture shows two distinct trends. In the hill country, the continuation of Iron Age traditions was still by far the most dominant factor. The coastal region, on the other hand, succumbed to the influences of western East-Greek, Cypriote and Attic elements as transmitted mainly by the Phoenicians, but also by Greek colonists. The material culture of the Greeks, therefore, appeared in Palestine long before the Macedonian conquest. The Persians themselves, however, seem to have left little permanent trace in the archaeological record apart from the occasional imported pottery type or item of metalwork of jewellery, many of which were in fact produced by the Phoenicians. Even the architecture of the period reflects little but the local traditions of the Iron Age. The fine palace or residency at Lachish, for example, contains not the slightest hint of Persian influence, but it is interesting to note again the clear Greek inspiration for the column bases of the entrance.

In 332 BC, following the battle of Issus, the vast empire of the Persians fell into the hands of Alexander the Great. Archaeologically, the event was to become a turning point, marked by the full-scale introduction of Greek culture and institutions. This process of Hellenism was to utterly transform the cities of ancient Palestine, providing them with the superficial appearance that many of them preserve to the present day. The material culture, which had developed and continued throughout the Bronze and Iron Ages, largely unaffected by the imposition of domination of external powers, was henceforth to become subservient to first Greek and then Roman ideals.

The political history of Palestine in the Hellenistic and Roman periods is relatively straightforward. Following the death of Alexander in 322 BC, and the bitter disputes for the succession amongst his generals, Palestine first came under the control of the Ptolemies of Egypt. The expansionist aims of the Ptolemies which, by the middle of the third century BC, had secured a circle of territory around the eastern Mediterranean, including Phoenicia, the southern coast of Anatolia, Cyrus and Aegean, brought them inevitably into conflict with the rival Syrian-based Dynasty, the Seleucids. In 200 BC Ptolemy V was defeated by Antiochus III at the battle of Panion, and Judah was annexed as part of the Seleucid empire. The changeover in power was seen by some as an opportunity to proclaim independence for Judah. The initial unrest that followed Antiochus III's capture of Jerusalem in 198 did not, however, develop into a full-scale rebellion, and had, in fact, a beneficial effect in that the Jews were granted certain tax concessions, and were assured of their rights to live according to their traditional laws.

The real trouble began after Antiochus III's death in 187 BC. Seleucus IV (187–175 BC) attempted to increase revenues from Jerusalem by taking treasures from the Temple. The high-priest, Onias, who resisted this attempt was deposed by his brother Jason, who, in return for high priestly office and Greek city status for Jerusalem, offered Antiochus IV (175–164 BC) increased tribute. Jason, however, was himself replaced by a financial official Menelaeus, who offended the Jewish community by selling off the Temple plate. Jason attempted to regain his former position by force, an act which was interpreted by Antiochus as a direct attack on Seleucid authority. Antiochus attacked Jerusalem in 167 BC and sacked and looted the Temple. He went much further, however, and issued a decree which effectively outlawed Jewish sacrifices, Sabbath observance, circumcision, and various other Jewish institutions. Greek cultic practices were not only introduced but were enforced, and the Temple of Jerusalem was in fact rededicated to Zeus.

Antiochus' decree led to an open revolt by the Jews, led initially by Judas ben Mattathias of the house of Hashmon. Following his death in 166 BC, the nationalist cause was taken up and developed by his son Judas, known as the 'Maccabee'. He and his successors, Jonathan and Simon, through a combination of military action and brilliant political manoeuvring, managed to throw off the Seleucid yoke, and to secure a brief period of independence for Judah (c.142–63 BC). The Hasmonaean monarchy effectively began with Simon (ruled 142–134 BC), who had negotiated with Demetrius II for Judah's exemption from tribute. The next fifty years saw the consolidation of Judah's position and its territoral expansion northwards into Samaria and Galilee, westwards to the coast, southwards to Idumaea and eastwards into Transjordan. Yet for all the successes of the Hasmonaeans, there were deeply rooted and fundamental problems with the basis of their monarchical power, for undisputed as their political leadership largely was, they assumed also the position of high-priest, an office for which they had no hereditary claim. Jonathan (died 143 BC) had been called the 'wicked priest' by the religiously devout community that had settled at Qumran in the middle of the second century BC. More overtly, Alexander Jannaeus (died 76 BC) had been pelted with lemons when he officiated as high-priest at the feast of Tabernacles. Alexander's reaction to this affront was to instigate a massacre of his opponents. The Pharisees called upon the Seleucid, Demetrius III, to deal with the Jannaeus, who reacted to this intervention by crucifying 800 opponents and killing their families. Following Jannaeus's death in 76 BC, the situation erupted into a civil war between his two sons, Hyrcanus (died 30 BC) and Aristobulus (died 49 BC) and one which was only finally resolved by Rome which, after many years of conflict had finally driven the Seleucids out of Syria. Between 67 and 63 BC Pompey campaigned in Asia Minor and under his 'Eastern Settlement', the Hasmonaean kingdom was reduced to the Roman provinces of Judaea and Idumaea. Aristobulus was defeated and deposed, and Hyrcanus was appointed as high-priest, but no longer king.

In 63 BC Pompey entered Jerusalem, and outraged the Jewish community by entering the Holy of Holies. Hycranus and his adviser, Antipater, were shrewd enough, however, to avoid a major conflict. Skilfully, too, they managed to walk the political tightrope during the struggle for power between Julius Caesar and Pompey, changing allegiance to the former at just the right time. It was in this way that Antipater's son Herod, at first an ally of Mark Anthony, and later as an ally of his victorious rival, Augustus, was appointed king of Judaea by the Roman Senate in 40 BC.

Under Herod's rule, Jerusalem was rebuilt – the citadel and a huge fortress, the Antonia, were created, and most important of all, the Temple was completely remodelled.

Herod died in 4 BC, and his son Archelaus proved to be entirely unsatisfactory as a ruler. He was dismissed and exiled by Augustus in AD 6 and Judaea became a province of the third class, administered by procurators. It was under the fifth of these Pontius Pilate (AD 27–30) that Jesus of Nazareth was put to death. During the reigns of Gaius (AD 37–41) and Claudius (AD 41–54), the policy of direct annexation was relaxed however, and, as a reward for loyalty, nearly all of the territory formerly ruled over by Herod the Great was returned to his grandson Herod Agrippa I. Unfortunately, Agrippa I died suddenly in AD 44 and since his son and heir was only seventeen years of age, Claudius transferred his entire kingdom to the control of a Roman procurator. Parts of the kingdom were handed back to Agrippa II in AD 53, and more territory was added during the reign of Nero (AD 54–68). It is probable that the entire extent of Agrippa I's kingdom would have been returned to his son had it not been for the revolt of the Jews in AD 66. This first revolt was only crushed after four years of bitter conflict, during which Jerusalem was laid siege to and subsequently destroyed. A second revolt occurred in AD 132 as a result of the Emperor Hadrian's (AD 117–137) decree prohibiting circumcision, and of his plan to build a Roman city on the site of Jerusalem. The rebellion, led by Simeon Bar Kokhba lasted for some three and a half years, and in the final phases took the form of a guerilla war in the Judaean desert. In the end, however, the rebellion was put down completely and severely. Hadrian's plan to build a Roman colony on the site of Jerusalem was put into effect. The name of Jerusalem was no more, and in its place arose Aelia Capitolina, now a pagan city inhabited by gentiles, and one which the Jews could not enter into, save only for once in the year on the anniversary of its destruction to lament at the site of the Temple.

Archaeological researches in Palestine have, for the Hellenistic and Roman periods, added a wealth of information to that already derived from the biblical and classical sources. Excavations at sites throughout the country have revealed the transformation wrought by the processes of Hellenism. Cities and towns were newly built or were remodelled along purely Greek lines, not only with regard to the individual buildings, but also in terms of the layout, and if any threat was posed to the process of Hellenism by the brief rule of a native Hasmonaean, it was averted by the arrival of the Romans, who ensured its continuation. During the Hellenistic and Roman periods there was a continuous development in architecture with later buildings being superimposed upon earlier ones. In most cases, therefore, the Hellenistic buildings have been totally eclipsed by later Roman constructions. An exception here is Tell Sandahanna, ancient Marissa, in south-western Palestine, which was destroyed by the Parthians in 40 BC and never rebuilt. The remains of the Hellenistic city were therefore preserved, and show very clearly the typical town layout, a planned grid with two main longitudinal north-south streets enclosing the agora, these being intersected by a number of cross-streets to create regular blocks.

Superficially, the towns and cities of Graeco-Roman Palestine must have appeared to have owed little to their rich culture heritage. Internally, however, many of the buildings, despite their outward appearances contained oriental features, both in terms of layout and, more importantly perhaps, with regard to decoration and ornamentation.

Perhaps the most impressive buildings constructed during the Hellenistic and Roman periods were those created by King Herod the Great towards the end of the first century BC. It is regrettable that excavations have revealed so little of what was undoubtedly Herod's greatest building achievement, the Temple in Jerusalem. Excavations at his palatial mountain-top, desert fortresses around the Jordan Valley and the Dead Sea have, however, revealed something of the splendour of his architecture. At Masada, which was later to become famous as the site of the Zealot's last stand in the first Jewish revolt, Herod

43. Limestone ossuary from Jerusalem. It is thought that the decoration imitates some well-known building, possibly the Temple of Herod, completed in AD 64. (BM WA 126392)

added to the existing Hasmonaean buildings a series of huge water cisterns, store-houses for food and ammunition, and a luxurious palace built on three natural rock terraces. The most remarkable of the desert fortresses, however, was at Herodium, where the whole of the lower part of the fortress was encased in an artificial mound to provide a quite extraordinary level of security. The fortress was, however, more than purely a military installation: Herod furnished it as a sumptuous palace.

Of all the discoveries made in the Graeco-Roman period, however, none can surely compare with that made in 1947 by an Arab goat-herd near the ruins of Khirbet Qumran. In pursuit of a runaway goat, he stumbled into a cave containing ancient Hebrew manuscripts. These manuscripts, now known as the 'Dead Sea Scrolls,' had been stored in cylindrical pottery jars, and are thought to have come from the library of Qumran, the monastery of an extremely religious group of Jews, the Essenes, who had moved to seclusion there in about 150 BC. The Scrolls, which are incomplete and fragmentary, must originally have included all of the Books of the Old Testament and the Apocrypha. Their value to biblical scholarship is immeasurable, being the earliest versions of the texts known so far. Excavations at the site of Khirbet Qumran yielded further valuable information regarding the Essenes and their monastery. It would seem that the site was destroyed by the Romans in AD 66–70 during the first Jewish revolt. Jars were found at Qumran similar to those used to contain the Scrolls, and a room has tentatively been identified as the library from which the Scrolls were taken shortly before the Roman attack in order to secrete them in the nearby caves for safekeeping. It is hard to conceive of a more appropriate or impressive tribute to the discipline of biblical archaeology than the discovery of the Dead Sea Scrolls.

44. Pottery jar with lid from Qumran, of the type used to contain the Dead Sea scrolls. (BM WA 131444)

Suggestions for Further Reading

Aharoni, Y.

1979 *The Land of the Bible: A Historical Geography.* 2nd revised edition. Philadelphia: Westminster Press.

Avi-Yonah, M. and Stern, E.

1975–8 *Encyclopedia of Archaeological Excavations in the Holy Land, I–IV.* London: Oxford University Press.

Finkelstein, I.

1988 *The Archaeology of the Israelite Settlement.* Jerusalem: Israel Exploration Society.

Hayes, J. H. and Miller, J. Maxwell (ed.)

1977 *Israelite and Judaean History.* London: SCM Press.

Kempinski, A. and Avi-Yonah, M.

1979 *Syria-Palestine II.* Archaeologia Mundi. Geneva: Nagel.

Kenyon, K. M.

1979 *Archaeology in the Holy Land.* 4th (revised) edition. London: Benn.

1987 *The Bible and Recent Archaeology.* Revised edition by P. R. S. Moorey. London: British Museum Publications.

Mitchell, T. C.

1988 *The Bible in the British Museum: Interpreting the Evidence.* London: British Museum Publications.

Pritchard, J. B. (ed.)

1987 *The Times Atlas of the Bible.* London: Times Books.

Thompson, T. L.

1974 *The Historicity of the Patriarchal Narratives: The Quest for the Historical Abraham.* Berlin: Walter de Gruyter.

Wright, G. E.

1962 *Biblical Archaeology.* Revised edition. London: Duckworth.

Chapter 4

Excavations at Tell es-Sa'idiyeh
Jonathan N. Tubb

The British Museum's current involvement with biblical archaeology is reflected in the excavations at Tell es-Sa'idiyeh in the east central Jordan Valley. The site, which is situated 1.8 km east of the River Jordan, on the south side of the Wadi Kufrinjeh, is composed of two elements: an Upper Tell to the east, which stands 14 m above present plain level and covers an area of about 10,000 sq m at the summit, and a low bench-like mound to the west, which measures approximately 90 m by 40 m, and is about 20 m lower than the upper mound. It stands as one of the most prominent landmarks in the central Jordan Valley, dominating some of the richest and most fertile agricultural land in the country.

Its size and position has obviously attracted speculation regarding an identification. Briefly, two major biblical candidates have been proposed and have gained some degree of acceptance. Firstly, *Zaphon*, which was proposed by Albright in 1926, largely on the basis of the reference in Judges 12 to the Ephraimites crossing the river Jordan to Zaphon in order to attack Jephthah. This view was more recently supported by Aharoni. In 1942 Nelson Glueck, having visited the site as part of his monumental survey of eastern Jordan, proposed instead *Zarethan*. This is mentioned in Joshua 3 in connection with the damming up of the Jordan to allow the Israelites to pass over. The text speaks of the waters being held back from Adamah (very plausibly identified as Tell ed-Damieh) as far as Zarethan. The city is further mentioned in an important reference in 1 Kings with regard to the casting of the copper vessels for use in Solomon's Temple in Jerusalem – they are said to have been cast in the plain between Succoth (Deir 'Alla) and Zarethan. Glueck also produced a late piece of corroborative evidence, a third century Talmudic source, which speaks of Adamah and Zarethan as being twelve miles apart. This is, in fact, the exact distance between Tell es-Sa'idiyeh and Tell ed-Damieh. On balance then, Zarethan is to be preferred, and this is the identification which has been accepted by the current expedition.

It was Nelson Glueck who visited Sa'idiyeh in the 1940s, who first drew attention to the enormous potential significance of the site. His surface collections indicated that Sa'idiyeh had a long sequence of occupation from at least the Early Bronze I until the Hellenistic period. About ten years later, in 1953, the French archaeologist Henri de Contensen conducted a small-scale excavation at Tell es-Sa'idiyeh el-Tahta, a very low mound lying to the west of the main double mound, and revealed there a thin occupation deposit associated with pottery and lithics of the Middle Chalcolithic period (fourth millennium BC).

It was not until 1964, however, that full-scale systematic excavations were begun at

Sa'idiyeh proper by a University of Pennsylvania expedition led by James Pritchard. During the course of four successive seasons, a number of areas on both the Upper and Lower Tells were investigated. On the Upper Tell, in the area which he called the 'acropolis', Pritchard revealed the plan of a palace of the Persian period. A number of important finds were uncovered, including a fine incense burner inscribed with the name *Zakur*. To the north and west, Pritchard opened up a very large area (1375 sq m) where he revealed four phases of the Iron Age city, dating between the seventh and ninth centuries BC. These showed a succession of rather insubstantially built industrial units, workshops and stores, arranged along well laid out streets and alleyways. By far the most impressive structure excavated by the Pennsylvania expedition on the upper mound, however, was the stone-built staircase on the north slope. The staircase had a mud-brick wall running along its centre, possibly to support a covering of beams. Pritchard believed that the staircase formed part of the city's water supply system, and had led to a spring at the base of mound. His excavations were, however, terminated before reaching the bottom of the steps.   On the Lower Tell, an area on the north side uncovered part of an extensive cemetery dating to the end of the Late Bronze and the beginning of the Iron Age (thirteenth to twelfth centuries BC). Many of the graves were found to be quite exceptionally rich. The cemetery was found to be cut into occupation of the Early Bronze Age which Pritchard, unfortunately, did not have time to investigate. The Pennsylvania excavations came to a close in 1967 with the war of that year, and for a variety of reasons, were not subsequently resumed. The results have now been published in final form in two excellent reports.

In 1985, with the encouragement of Professor Pritchard and the Department of Antiquities of Jordan, the writer applied for, and was generously granted a permit to resume

45. Tell es-Sad'idiyeh from the north, showing the Upper Tell on the left and the Lower Tell on the right. The Wadi Kufrinjeh is in the centre ground, marked by the line of oleanders. (photo: JNT)

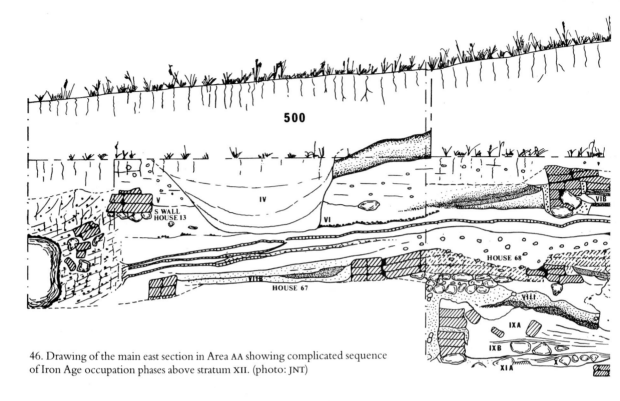

46. Drawing of the main east section in Area AA showing complicated sequence of Iron Age occupation phases above stratum XII. (photo: JNT)

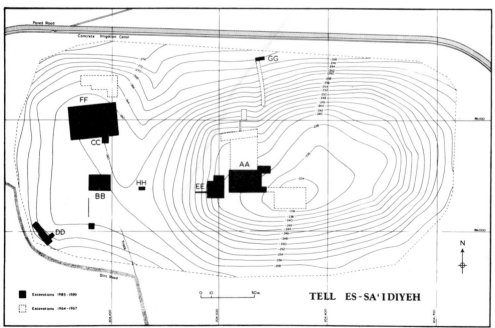

47. Contour plan of Tell es-Saʿidiyeh showing excavated areas. (photo: JNT)

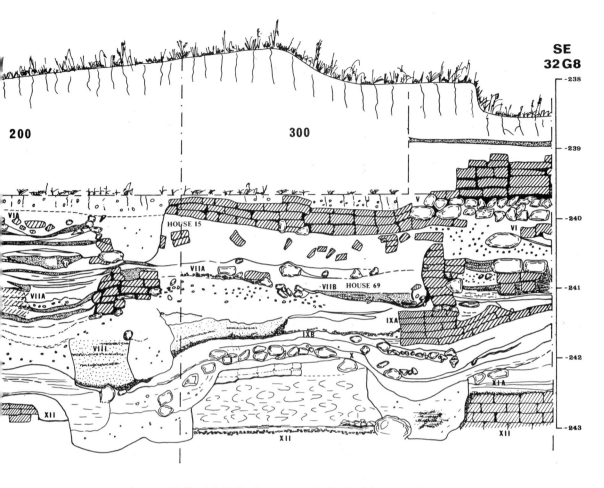

excavations at Tell es-Sa'idiyeh, now on behalf of the British Museum. Five major seasons of excavations have taken place since 1985, in the last two of which, in 1989 and 1990, the British Museum has been joined by the Rijksmuseum van Oudheden as a participating contributor, an arrangement which has enabled the scale of operations to be greatly increased.

Excavations on the Upper Tell

Area AA, situated in the southern part of Pritchard's large trench of the 1960s, is intended to continue the sequence of occupational phases below the lowermost reached by the Pennsylvania team, stratum VII, an Iron Age city level dating to the late ninth to early eighth century BC. In 1985, when this area was initiated, Pritchard's excavation report had not yet been published, and it was not appreciated that the southern part of his trench had not in fact been excavated down to stratum VII, but had been left in 1967 at some point during the isolation of stratum VI on the eastern side, with deeper soundings into and indeed below stratum VII on the west. Much of the work was initially concerned, therefore, with the definition and isolation of residual deposit attributable to stratum

VI, followed by the complete excavation of stratum VII. As far as stratum VI is concerned, very little can be said; the remains were too eroded to allow anything of value to be added to the plan published by Pritchard for the area to the north. One observation is, however, of interest and that is that stratum VI must have represented a small and quite sparse settlement, nucleated towards the centre of the Tell's surface. No trace of VI was found on the western side of AA, and as if to reinforce this point, what was found there was a burial, stratigraphically clearly belonging to stratum VI, and in a context in which it must be seen as having been extramural. Interestingly, the peculiar postures of the two individuals in the burial, suggest that they might have been executions rather than routine interments.

Below the rather miserable remnants of stratum VI, extensive and well-preserved remains of stratum VI have been found all over area AA, and have substantial architectural features and details can be added to the plan published by Pritchard for the area to the north. A whole series of houses and courtyards have been excavated, arranged along narrow streets paved with a mixture of pebbles and sherds. An interesting feature is that the external house walls were provided with raised footings to prevent the foundations from being washed out, and high thresholds reduced the risk of the rooms being flooded. Many of the houses contained internal installations such as mud-brick baths, bins, ovens and pits. However, one of the main activities, perhaps even on an industrial scale, seems to have been weaving and textile preparation. Many of the rooms contained large numbers of loom weighs, often in distinctive alignments suggesting the configuration of the looms. Most of the pottery from stratum VII consists of large vessels – kraters, storejars, pithoi and cooking pots, and only very few finer pieces have been found.

Excavations in area AA have also confirmed Pritchard's subdivision of VII into two subphases, VIIA the later and VIIB the earlier. Again, by virtue of excavating over a wider area, it has been possible to add a further dimension to this purely chronological sequence. For it is now clear that VIIB, the original phase, represents a fairly sparse but well-constructed settlement with large rooms and countyards, but perhaps not very extensive. Certainly it did not reach to the edge of the Tell. Subphase VIIA, characterised by the use of a distinctive orange-coloured mud-brick can now be seen to represent the result of a substantial building programme creating extensive additions to the VIIB plan. The settlement of VIIA clearly reached to the edge of the mound, where in area EE (see below) it is seen to be confined by a perimeter wall associated with a stone-paved walkway. Most of the VIIB rooms showed evidence of having been partitioned, and many of the individual VIIB walls were rebuilt or patched up. The homogeneous nature of the VIIA additions suggests a quite rapid process of building, perhaps indicative of a population ingress at the beginning of the eighth century BC. It is possible that this revitalisation of the settlement is related to the activities of Jeroboam II, king of Israel, who is known to have re-established authority over Transjordan as far as the Dead Sea (II Kings 14: 28).

Below stratum VII, excavations in 1986–7 on the eastern side of area AA, revealed a complicated sequence of earlier occupations, the complexity of which can best be appreciated from the drawing of the main east section (see fig. 46). Generally, these phases (i.e. VIII–X) appear to be rather poor, and in the area excavated, were dominated by a series of roughly paved cobbled courtyards associated with refuse pits. It was not until stratum XIA which can be dated to the eleventh century BC, that more substantial architectural remains were encountered. Although greatly disrupted by later building activities, the plan was recovered of a sizeable two-roomed building with carefully laid mud-brick floors. The overall plan of the building, together with various internal details, such as a plastered bench against the rear wall with an inset niche, suggest a possible interpretation for this building as a small temple.

Stratum XI was built over a massive levelling fill of mud-brick rubble and pisée, which had been laid over the burnt-out ruins of stratum XII. This important and widespread destruction level was partially excavated in 1986 with the clearance of a single room. In 1987 the area was expanded and the plan emerged of a substantial and impressive public building, consisting of storerooms, courtyards and stepped passageways. The dis-

48. Overhead view of Egyptian Governor's Residency in Area AA (twelfth century BC). (photo: JNT)

covery of this building has proved to be of major significance, for the unusual plan can be paralleled exactly by a group of buildings found in Palestine which are known as 'Egyptian Governors Residences'. They occur at sites such as Beth Shan, Tell el-Far'ah, and Tell Sera, which were major administrative centres for the Egyptian control of Canaan during the New Kingdom. All of them, including the one at Sa'idiyeh, are characterised by a peculiarly Egyptian construction method which utilises deeply laid brick foundations rather than the usual stone, and has external walls built as pairs with a channel between them in order to accommodate an effective drainage system. The stratum XII building was destroyed around 1150 BC, and the metre and a half or so of destruction debris not only served to preserve the walls to this height, but also sealed a rich corpus of complete pottery vessels and other objects, many of which show strong Egyptian influence.

As mentioned above, the complicated series of rather poor occupation phases between stratum VII and stratum XII were defined in 1986–8 on the eastern side of area AA. In the 1989 season, it became clear that, as in the case of stratum VI, these were not extensive settlement phases. None of them appeared to have reached the edge of the Tell, for certainly on the western side of area AA, stratum XII lies directly below VII.

This same situation has also been found in area EE on the western side of the Tell, an area started in 1986 with the intention of studying the defences of the site. Here,

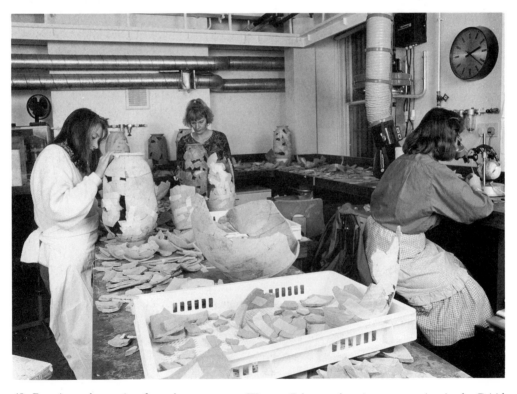

49. Egyptian-style storejars from the stratum XII Western Palace undergoing conservation in the British Museum's laboratories. (BM)

50. Overhead view of the twelfth-century BC water system staircase, showing the lowermost steps and semi-circular pool. (photo: JNT)

beneath some heavily eroded structures attributable to stratum V, and the perimeter wall belonging to stratum VII, was found the dense, heavily burnt destruction debris of stratum XII.

Removal of this thick deposit revealed the remains of a truly massive 6m-thick solid city wall, and extending behind it a second major public building, which for the sake of argument may be described as a palace complex. Again, as in the case of the Residency building in area AA, this building shows purely Egyptian building techniques, with deep brick foundations and no use of stone. Again are found the same use of channel walls, and, in the case of the palace, even the individual bricks correspond precisely in size with those of Egyptian New Kingdom buildings.

One of the rooms had a floor finely paved with mud-bricks, and to the west of this were two partially sunken rooms which appear to represent a type of bath complex. Both rooms were thickly plastered and the slight incurving of the preserved wall tops suggests that they might have been vaulted. A small tunnel connected the eastern room to the western, which lay at a lower level, and which had at its base a clearly defined water channel and an exit conduit. Significantly, in view of the Egyptian nature of the architecture, the lower room contained a clay sealing from a papyrus roll, the texture of the papyrus and the impression of the string tie clearly visible on the reverse. Elsewhere in the palace complex, the heavily burnt floor surfaces produced good collections of typical mid-twelfth century pottery.

One of the rooms had a thickly plastered floor which had been laid on a deliberate slope, facing a diagonally placed pisée wall. The floor, which showed evidence for extensive water channelling, was covered with sherds of Egyptian storejars, perhaps representing as many as fifty or sixty complete vessels, and it is possible that this unusual room had been used as a sort of water cooling reservoir, perhaps for wine storage.

One of the major undertakings of the 1987 season was the further examination of Pritchard's staircase on the north slope. This structure, which can now also be related to stratum XII, had been left unfinished by the Pennsylvania expedition. In 1987, therefore, the staircase was re-excavated and the work was then continued in depth, revealing further steps. At a depth of some 6 m below present plain level, water was reached, and it was possible to define the structure of an enclosed pool. Prichard's theory that the staircase was an element of a water system has certainly been shown to be correct, and it was quite a sophisticated one too, with the water issuing through a conduit on the south side, and draining through a channel on the north. Although not specifically Egyptian in design, this water system is equally non Canaanite, and it is interesting to observe that its closest parallels are to be found at Mycenae and Tiryns.

Excavations on the Lower Tell

A further important dimension can be added to our understanding of stratum XII, for excavations on the Lower Tell have uncovered part of the extensive and intensively used cemetery contemporary with this settlement. In area BB, which lies towards the centre of the Lower Tell, some 340 graves have so far been excavated. A few of these, perhaps less than ten per cent, belong to the Iron III/Persian period, and can be related to the Persian phase of occupation represented by stratum III on the Upper Tell. The majority of the graves, however, belong to the thirteenth and twelfth centuries BC, contemporary, that is, with stratum XII on the Upper Tell.

Many of the graves have been grossly disturbed through the effects of intensive re-use of the same area, but despite this, it has been possible to assemble a substantial corpus of well-preserved burials. They show considerable variation with regard to grave construction, disposition of the deceased, burial practice and grave goods, suggestive indeed of a mixed population. Many of the graves consist of simple pits, some of which have

51. Grave 65, a child's burial of the twelfth century BC. (photo: JNT)

made use of Early Bronze Age architectural elements from the underlying occupation layers – foundation stones, fragments of walling, and even re-used structural mud-bricks.

Several of the graves were more elaborately constructed from mud-brick slabs and were roofed over with the same material. Some of these were clearly intended to be partially visible above ground level, being more in the nature of tombs rather than graves.

One of the most important burial types found at Sa'idiyeh is the so-called 'Double Pithos' burial, in which the body was contained within a pottery 'coffin' composed of two very large storejars joined shoulder to shoulder. Grave goods were placed both inside and around the outside of the pithoi, and, for the most part, these were strongly Egyptian in character. This type of burial, which is elsewhere extremely rare in Palestine, is now well represented in the Sa'idiyeh cemetery, with over twenty examples. Its occurrence may well indicate the presence of a Sea Peoples element within the population, for the functional similarity between the Double Pithos container and the anthropoid clay coffin, known to have been used by the Philistines, seems undeniable. A somewhat poorer expression of the same practice has also been found in a number of graves, where the head of the deceased only was placed inside the storejar, the rest of the body being covered with large sherds. Small storejars were frequently used as burial containers for infants, the jar having been cut off at the neck in order to insert the body.

Generally, the burial practice was single and primary. A few examples of double or multiple burials have been found, but quite a common finding is what may be described

52. (*right*) Bronze wine set from Grave 32. (BM WA Z86 T32. 1–3/ photo: JNT)

53. (*below*) Grave 46, a late thirteenth-century burial containing a rich assemblage of bronzes, jewellery and pottery vessels. (photo: JNT)

54. Grave 251 (twelfth century BC). The textile remains preserved on the javelin and the tightly drawn up shoulders seen in the posture of the deceased together indicate that the body had been bound in a wrapping of Egyptian linen. (photo: JNT)

as a 'derived secondary' practice. This may be seen as a function of the extreme intensity of usage of the same cemetery area over a period of time. During the digging of graves it must not have been an uncommon event to have disturbed a previous interment. In such cases, in order to show some degree of respect, the skull, and often a couple of the long bones, were carefully retrieved and were placed inside the new grave. In grave 32 for example, in addition to the principle interment, which was associated with a beautiful three-piece bronze wine set, no less than four other skulls had been included.

In terms of grave goods, the Sa'idiyeh cemetery is a rich one, arguing for an affluent and sophisticated society. The graves have produced rich assemblages of pottery, metalwork, stone vessels, ivory and jewellery, many of which show strong Egyptian influence, or are indeed purely Egyptian. Not only are many of the grave goods Egyptian in character, but so too are some of the somewhat unusual burial practices. In several instances a pottery, or more usually a bronze, bowl had been placed over the face of the deceased, and examples have also been found in which the genitals have been covered with a bowl. This extraordinary practice can be paralleled at the Egyptian New Kingdom cemetery of Bubastis in the Delta. Another practice, also paralleled at Bubastis, is the ritual killing of weapons. Daggers in particular, but also javelins and arrowheads, were bent almost double before deposition in the grave. This practice was not, however, confined solely to metal weapons: many of the pottery vesels included in the graves had had a tiny piece taken out of the rim, again as part of a ritual killing process.

The majority of the bronze objects found in the graves (vessels, weapons, pins and other items of jewellery) were found to be covered in textile remains. Examination of these materials has demonstrated that in every case so far examined, they consist of Egyptian linen. In some instances the evidence would suggest that the objects had been wrapped in cloth and deposited separately, but in others it is clear that they were incorporated in a tight binding around the body. Even when bronze objects were not included amongst the grave offerings, the process of binding is often suggested by the posture of the deceased. In several cases, the shoulders are tightly drawn up, or the arms are drawn across the chest, or the feet are crossed over. The Egyptian character of these bound burials hardly needs pointing out. Even more remarkable, however, has been the finding of traces of a black bituminous material over the bones of some of the burials. This may even imply that some attempt at mummification was being made.

The intensity of usage of the cemetery area, producing considerable disruption to the graves through the effects of repeated intercutting, has had one important result, in that it has allowed for the development of an internal chronology based on linked sequences of graves. From the data retrieved so far, it has been possible to define four main phases of cemetery usage for the Late Bronze III period, during the second of which some type of building was constructed in the cemetery area. Due to the subsequent

55. Ivory cosmetic box in the form of a fish and bronze bowl from Grave 232 (late thirteenth century BC). (BM WA Z87 T232. 1–2/ photo: JNT)

digging of graves in phases 3 and 4, few traces have survived, and no indication as to its nature or function can be given. It is interesting to note, however, that the construction method yet again shows the characteristically Egyptian techniques found in the public buildings of the Upper Tell. Directly below the deep brick foundations of the south wall of this building was found a burial. The proximity of the lowest course of brickwork to the skull was such that it would have been impossible to have inserted burial without disrupting the wall, and quite impossible to have put in the wall without damaging the skull. The conclusion must be, therefore, that the building and the burial were purely contemporaneous and were directly associated with one another. In another words, the burial appears to have been a type of foundation deposit. The burial itself was quite exceptional, for the body had been intered, usually, face down. Over the back of the skull were found two fish skeletons, and over the genitals had been placed a bronze bowl which, when emptied of its soil, revealed an outstanding ivory cosmetic box in the form of a fish.

The Early Bronze Age Occupation on the Lower Tell

The original intention in laying out area BB in 1985 was to provide a good sized area for the examination of the Early Bronze Age occupation which was known to have been present on the Lower Tell from the excavations of Pritchard. Now that much of the area has been cleared of graves the fragmentary and grossly disturbed remains of this occupation are starting to be revealed. Two superimposed architectural phases have been isolated, the uppermost associated with an extensive and intense destruction. Fortunately, the key to our understanding of these two poorly preserved phases, to which the stratum numbers L2 and L3 have been assigned, has been provided by excavations in area DD which lies on the southwest corner of the Tell. Here, between 1985 and 1978, the Early Bronze Age occupation was examined in an area which appeared to lie beyond the limits of the later cemetery. The uppermost stratum, L2, had suffered badly from erosion, but it was possible, nevertheless, to salvage the plan of a two-roomed building, constructed of mud-brick on well-laid stone foundations with carefully prepared white plaster floors. This phase had ended in a destruction, and the thick deposit of debris consisting of burnt mud-brick and ashes served to seal a rich and varied assemblage of crushed but complete pottery vessels. Examination of the pottery would place stratum L2 and its destruction towards the end of the Early Bronze II period, around 2700 BC. Many of the vessels are decorated in a distinctive 'ribbon-painted' style, and the repertoire includes many innovative features such as four-spouted lamps: these do not regularly occur in the Levant until the Early Bronze IV period, some 300 years later. Rather conveniently, the brickwork of stratum L2 is peculiar and rather distinctive, being light greyish green in colour. It has been possible to detect it quite easily, therefore, in area BB, even in the most fragmentary and disturbed states. There, too, it is associated with an extensive destruction horizon, and combining the evidence from the two areas it is clear that stratum L2 represents the final phase of habitation on the Lower Tell.

Below stratum L2 in area DD, excavations have revealed the better preserved architecture of stratum L3. This phase, which was found to be on the same alignment as L2, was built using bricks of a completely different colour: deep orange brown, and again, this distinctive brickwork can be detected in area BB where it also directly underlies stratum L2. In area DD it has been possible to recover a coherent plan of stratum L3, showing a rectangular building with an attached courtyard, a pebble-paved street, and part of another building on the other side of the street. The house floors were relatively clean, but enough pottery was recovered to show that this stratum lies also within the Early Bronze II period. A number of large storejars had been set into the floors with stones or sherds as covers. Analysis of the residue on the interior of one of these jars produced the result – olive oil. The removal of the jars has also provided the opportunity to examine the underlying stratigraphy, from which is clear there are at least three more phases of Early Bronze Age occupation below stratum L3.

The first of these, stratum L4 has started to be examined in area BB. In one of the squares, now completely clear of graves, excavations in 1989 revealed a complicated series of mud-brick paved platforms and sunken rooms, associated in one part with a thick, 20 cm or so, horizon of mineralised grape and fig seeds. Such a finding is fully

56. Part of a well-preserved Early Bronze II house (stratum L2) containing a fine deposit of pottery vessels. (photo: JNT)

57. Overhead view of stratum L3 house with associated street in Area DD. (photo: JNT)

compatible with what is known of the Early Bronze Age economy, suggesting that wine was being produced possibly for export to Egypt.

The Tell es-Sa'idiyeh excavation project will continue for several more seasons. Already, however, the excavations have made a major contribution to our understanding of the nature and extent of the Egyptian control of Canaan during the latter part of the New Kingdom empire, a period which, as we have seen in chapter 3, was of vital importance in the formation and development of the Israelite nation. For the results have clearly shown that Sa'idiyeh was a major Egyptian centre in the Twentieth Dynasty.

Why then should an Egyptian centre have been established at Sa'idiyeh, east of the River Jordan, during the final phase of the empire? The answer to this question almost certainly lies in the position of the site, for Sa'idiyeh is situated on the south side of the Wadi Kufrinjeh, very close to the Jordan river, and immediately east of a wide and extremely shallow ford. This ford had in fact been recorded during the Survey of Western Palestine, but seems to have been subsequently overlooked until it was rediscovered during the 1986 season. The River Jordan would have presented, therefore, no barrier to communication between east and west, and in these terms, Sa'idiyeh can be seen as an eastern extension of Egypt's network of administrative centres in Canaan. The importance of these findings should not, however, be over-extrapolated, for the discoveries made cannot and should not be used to suggest extensive Egyptian control of Transjordan at this time. Rather, Sa'idiyeh should be seen as a localised and perhaps even quite isolated outpost of the Egyptian empire. Its function was probably specific. Despite its massive fortifications, complete with concealed water system, it would seem unlikely that Sa'idiyeh's role was strategic in a strictly military sense. It seems more reasonable to suggest that its importance was primarily economic, serving as a trading entrepôt or taxation centre. In this capacity, the location of the site was ideal, for not only does Sa'idiyeh lie at the heart of the most extensive alluvial fan east of the Jordan, commanding some of the richest and most fertile agricultural land in the country, but also it had immediate access to the equally important hinterland to the east. The valley of the Kufrinjeh leads back to the area that divides very roughly, the hill country of Gilead, renowned for its wines, and the well-watered plateau south of Bashan, noted for its cattle.

That such commodities as wine, olive oil, agricultural produce and cattle were in great demand in Egypt is certainly clear from the temple lists in papyrus Harris, and these lists do refer to produce received from 'Syria', that is, in the wider sense, including Palestine. Sa'idiyeh has yet another considerable advantage. It lies at the narrowest neck of the valley, at a point where the Ghor is no more than 4 km wide. An east–west route across the Jordan at Sa'idiyeh would have had a number of clear advantages, for not only would it have involved the shortest valley crossing, but it would also have avoided the bad lands topography further south, which is virtually impassable in wet weather. This factor would have been of particular value, of course, if the crossing had involved animals. Camels, and especially laden camels, are helpless on a slippery surface and are quite unable, or unwilling, to enter a stream from a muddy bank. Altogether then, it would seem most likely that the Egyptians were attracted to Sa'idiyeh because of its geographical setting. The ford west of the Tell provided easy access to the much-needed commodities of the east central Jordan Valley and its hinterland, and Sa'idiyeh was developed as a major trade entrepôt serving the needs of the empire in its final phase.

More detailed preliminary reports on the excavations at Tell es-Sa'idiyeh are published in the journal, *Levant*: Vol. XX (1988) for the first three seasons, Vol. XXII (1990) for the fourth (1989) season, and Vol. XXIII (1991) for the fifth (1990) season.

Chronology

Egypt		Palestine		Mesopotamia
	8000 BC		8000 BC	
		Pre-Pottery Neolithic A		
	7350 BC		7350 BC	
Epipaleolithic	7000 BC		7000 BC	
		Pre-Pottery Neolithic B		Jarmo
				Nineveh I–II
	6000 BC		6000 BC	
	5500 BC		5500 BC	
		Pottery Neolithic A		Halafian
	4500 BC		4500 BC	
		Pottery Neolithic B		
	4200 BC		4200 BC	
Badarian		Ghassul-Beersheba Culture		Ubaid
Naqada I				
	3500 BC		3500 BC	
Naqada II, Fayum B, and		Proto-Urban		Uruk
Ma'adi Cultures	3100 BC		3100 BC	
1st Dynasty		Early Bronze Age I		Jamdat Nassr (Uruk III)
				Early Dynastic I
Narmer (c.3100 BC)	2800 BC		2800 BC	
2nd Dynasty		Early Bronze Age II		Early Dynastic II
	2600 BC		2600 BC	
3rd Dynasty		Early Bronze Age III		Early Dynastic III
4th Dynasty				Gilgamesh of Uruk
5th Dynasty				(c.2600 BC)
6th Dynasty		Early Bronze Age IV		Dynasty of Akkad
	2180 BC		2180 BC	
7th–10th Dynasties				Gutian Interregnum
	2112 BC		2112 BC	
11th Dynasty				IIIrd Dynasty of Ur
12th Dynasty		Middle Bronze IIA		Isin–Larsa Period
	1870 BC		1870 BC	
				1st Dynasty of Babylon
				(1870–1531 BC)
				Hammurabi
13th–14th, and 16th		Middle Bronze IIB–C		(c.1768–1726 BC)
Dynasties				
15th and 17th Dynasties				Kassite Period
				(1600–1200 BC)
	1550 BC		1550 BC	
18th Dynasty		Late Bronze I		
Ahmose (1570–1546 BC)				
Amenohotpe I (1546–1526 BC)				
Tuthmosis I (1525–1512 BC)				
Tuthmosis II (1512–1504 BC)				
Hatshepsut (1503–1482 BC)				
Tuthmosis III (1504–1450 BC)				
Amenophis II (1450–1425 BC)				
Tuthmosis IV (1425–1417 BC)				
Amenophis III (1417–1379 BC)	1400 BC		1400 BC	
Akhenaton (1379–1362 BC)		Late Bronze IIA		

Chronology *continued*

Egypt		Palestine			Mesopotamia
Seti I (1318–1304 BC) 19th Dynasty Ramesses II (1304–1237 BC)	1300 BC	Late Bronze IIB		1300 BC	
Merneptah (1236–1223 BC) 20th Dynasty Ramesses III (1198–1166 BC)	1200 BC	Late Bronze III		1200 BC	Middle Assyrian and Middle Babylonian Periods (1200–750 BC)
	1150 BC	Iron Age I		1150 BC	
21st Dynasty					
22nd Dynasty	1000 BC	Saul (1030–1000 BC) Iron Age II David (1000–960 BC)		1000 BC	Neo-Assyrian Empire
Sheshonq I (945–924 BC)		Solomon (960–931 BC)			
		Judah	*Israel*		
		Rehoboam (931–913 BC) Abijah (913–911 BC) Asa (911–870 BC) Jehoshaphat (870–848 BC)	Jeroboam I (931–910 BC) Omri (885–874 BC) Ahab (874–853 BC) Jehu (841–814 BC)		Ashurnasirpal II (884–859 BC)
		Hezekiah (716–687 BC) Josiah (641–609 BC) Kingdom destroyed (587/6 BC)	Jeroboam II (782–753 BC) Kingdom destroyed (722 BC)		Tiglath-pileser III (745–727 BC) Shalmaneser V (727–722 BC) Sargon (722–705 BC) Sennacherib (705–681 BC)
23rd–26th Dynasties	587/6 BC	Neo-Babylonian Empire		587/6 BC	Nebuchadnezzar (605–562 BC)
	539 BC	Persian Empire		539 BC	Persian Empire
Persian Empire					
Alexander the Great	332 BC	Alexander the Great		332 BC	Alexander the Great
	323 BC			323 BC	
Ptolemaic Dynasty		Ptolemaic Empire Seleucid Empire Hasmonean Dynasty (142–63 BC)			Seleucid Dynasty
	63 BC	Roman Empire Herod the Great (37–4 BC) Herod Antipas (4 BC–AD 39) Agrippa I (AD 40–44)		63 BC	